ROUTLEDGE LIBRARY EDITIONS: ETHICS

Volume 38

ETHICS, PERSUASION AND TRUTH

ETHICS, PERSUASION AND TRUTH

J.J.C. SMART

LONDON AND NEW YORK

First published in 1984 by Routledge & Kegan Paul Ltd

This edition first published in 2021
by Routledge
2 Park Square, Milton Park, Abingdon, Oxon OX14 4RN

and by Routledge
52 Vanderbilt Avenue, New York, NY 10017

Routledge is an imprint of the Taylor & Francis Group, an informa business

© 1984 J. J. C. Smart & Others. Please see original copyright page

All rights reserved. No part of this book may be reprinted or reproduced or utilised in any form or by any electronic, mechanical, or other means, now known or hereafter invented, including photocopying and recording, or in any information storage or retrieval system, without permission in writing from the publishers.

Trademark notice: Product or corporate names may be trademarks or registered trademarks, and are used only for identification and explanation without intent to infringe.

British Library Cataloguing in Publication Data
A catalogue record for this book is available from the British Library

ISBN: 978-0-367-85624-3 (Set)
ISBN: 978-1-00-305260-9 (Set) (ebk)
ISBN: 978-0-367-50765-7 (Volume 38) (hbk)
ISBN: 978-1-00-305117-6 (Volume 38) (ebk)

Publisher's Note
The publisher has gone to great lengths to ensure the quality of this reprint but points out that some imperfections in the original copies may be apparent.

Disclaimer
The publisher has made every effort to trace copyright holders and would welcome correspondence from those they have been unable to trace.

Ethics, Persuasion and Truth

J.J.C. Smart

ROUTLEDGE & KEGAN PAUL
London, Boston, Melbourne and Henley

To Elizabeth

First published in 1984
by Routledge & Kegan Paul plc
14 Leicester Square, London WC2H 7PH, England
9 Park Street, Boston, Mass. 02108, USA
464 St Kilda Road, Melbourne,
Victoria 3004, Australia and
Broadway House, Newtown Road,
Henley-on-Thames, Oxon RG9 1EN, England

Set in Times Roman
by Columns, Reading
and printed in Great Britain
by St Edmundsbury Press Ltd,
Bury St Edmunds, Suffolk

Chapter 2, pages 22-34, © 1982 by D. Reidel
Publishing Company, Dordrecht, Holland
Chapter 3 © 1982 by Verlag Anton Hain KG, Meisenheim/Glan
Chapter 7 © 1984 by Verlag Königshausen und Neumann, Würzburg
Chapter 8, pages 128-38, © The Royal Institute of Philosophy 1981
All other material © J.J.C. Smart 1984

No part of this book may be reproduced in
any form without permission from the publisher,
except for the quotation of brief passages
in criticism

ISBN 0-7102-0245-8

CONTENTS

	Preface	vii
	Acknowledgments	ix
I	Introduction	1
II	Interlude on the naturalistic fallacy	22
III	Why moral language?	45
IV	Considerations about the semantics of 'ought'	64
V	Goodness	82
VI	Ethics, truth and fact	94
VII	'Ought', 'can', free will and responsibility	106
VIII	Ethics, science and metaphysics	128
	Notes	144
	Index	156

PREFACE

Though in the past my concerns in ethics have been largely in *normative* ethics, in particular in defending a form of utilitarianism, this book is on *meta-ethics*, i.e. *about* rather than *in* ethics. It is therefore meant to be prescriptively neutral, though here and there my normative predilections are discernible. Most books on meta-ethics depend very much on the notions of meaning and analyticity. For reasons made familiar by Professor W.V. Quine I try to eschew these notions, or at any rate to make minimal use of them, or to use them as in part of Chapter 2 merely for the sake of argument against those who do use them. This austerity seems to me to be philosophically necessary, though as a result meta-ethics has revealed itself to me as more difficult than I used to think it was. This book could be said to be mostly on the semantics and pragmatics of ethical language, with some emphasis on the latter. In the final two chapters I relate these matters to questions of free will and of relations between ethics on the one hand and science and metaphysics on the other hand.

Some of the chapters are partly based, with omissions, additions and alterations, on papers that have been published in journals, and in the case of Chapter 7, in a volume of essays edited by Professor B. Kanitscheider of the Justus-Liebig Universität, Giessen. Detailed acknowledgments are made on page xi.

I am grateful to Professor Bruce Vermazen for his kindness in commenting on parts of Chapters 4 and 6 in which I expound some of his interesting ideas on the semantics of the practical

Preface

'ought'. Errors of exposition that may remain should not be attributed to him. Professor R.M. Hare very kindly and patiently read an earlier draft of the typescript. He made many helpful suggestions and saved me from some bad errors. In spite of this he will still profoundly disagree with my treatment of some central issues in this book, especially because of my Quinean bias on the analytic-synthetic distinction and my use of pragmatic considerations in places where he would say that they are out of place. I am extremely grateful for his valuable comments.

In 1979 from January to July inclusive I was fortunate to be a Fellow at the Center for Advanced Study in the Behavioral Sciences, Stanford. I should like to express my thanks to the Center, its Director, and other friends there, for a happy and stimulating time in which I did some of the preliminary thinking about this book.

I should like to express my thanks to Mrs Mitzi Parkins for her help in typing this book and making all sorts of belated corrections to the typescript without losing her cheerfulness, and to Mrs Jean Norman who looked up and checked a number of references while I was abroad.

J.J.C.S
Canberra and St Andrews
October, 1983

ACKNOWLEDGMENTS

Much of Chapter 2 is taken from my article 'Prior and the basis of ethics', *Synthese 53* (1982), pp. 3-17, published by D. Reidel Publishing Company, Dordrecht, Holland.

Most of Chapter 3 is taken from my article 'Why moral language?', *Zeitschrift für Philosophische Forschung 36* (1982), pp. 153-68, published by Verlag Anton Hain KG, Meisenheim/Glan.

Much of Chapter 7 is taken from my article 'Physikalismus und Willensfreiheit', in B. Kanitscheider (editor), *Moderne Naturphilosophie* (1984), published by Verlag Königshausen und Neumann, Würzburg.

Much of Chapter 8 is taken from my article 'Ethics and science', *Philosophy 56* (1981), pp. 449-65, published by Cambridge University Press. This article was a Martineau Memorial Lecture given at the University of Tasmania and published as a pamphlet by the University of Tasmania in 1981 (University of Tasmania Occasional Paper 30).

I wish to express my thanks to all the publishers and editors concerned.

I

INTRODUCTION

FIRST ORDER QUESTIONS AND SECOND ORDER QUESTIONS

In this book I wish to discuss certain questions that are *about* ethics rather than *in* ethics. I shall not here be concerned to advocate a method of making concrete ethical decisions or to propose a rule or set of rules for conduct, though I have done something of this sort elsewhere.[1] I shall be concerned with questions about the semantics and pragmatics of ethical thinking. Thus for the most part I shall be concerned with 'second order' questions, not with 'first order' ethical questions, such as, for example, whether it could ever be right to wage a nuclear war, whether abortion is right or wrong, or whether we should approve of certain practices of factory farming. The just-mentioned examples of first order questions are examples of rather general questions, but of course one must not forget the vast array of quite particular first order questions, for example as to whether a certain person, who is out of work and has to provide for a family, ought to accept an offer of a public relations post in aid of a political party with an abhorrent social programme.

Though one can make a rough division into first order questions and second order questions, it is important not to prejudge the question of whether this division is in the end a neat and exclusive one. In the period of British analytic philosophy just after the Second World War it was often assumed that there

1

Introduction

was such a neat division. The pursuit of first order ethical discourse was thought of as something like preaching, at which philosophers have no special competence or expertise. Analytic philosophers claimed a different sort of competence. This was to investigate the meanings of first order ethical sentences, to clarify ethical concepts, such as that of 'duty' or of 'rights' or of 'virtue', and to answer such questions as that of whether statements of what we ought to do could be deduced purely from questions of scientific fact. It was conceded that such activity might have some effect on practical morality, since a moralist might modify his recommendations in the light of a second order or conceptual investigation, if he became convinced that his ethical reasoning had been distorted by muddleheadedness.

For example in undergraduate courses on moral philosophy, the students may be introduced to the elementary distinction between the rightness of an act and the goodness of the motive from which the act was done. A college is electing a president. Smith is arguing for the merits of Green. Brown says to Jones that they should not vote for Green because Smith's advocacy of Green is motivated almost entirely by Smith's envy and dislike of Green's rival candidate Robinson. If Jones had some training in philosophy (and perhaps even without, as I am using a rather simple example) he might point out to Brown the distinction between the rightness or wrongness of an act and the goodness or badness of the motive from which it sprang. Smith's advocacy of Green was from a bad motive, but he might have been right to advocate Green all the same.

So conceptual clarification might have some slight practical value. Nevertheless, on the whole, analytic philosophers tended to play down the practical consequences for morality of second order or conceptual investigations. (I am here of course describing a general climate of opinion, and there were of course analytic philosophers, notably R.M. Hare, with a passionate interest in practical moral questions, and in the reciprocal interplay between conceptual and practical reasoning.) Moral philosophy was thought of as rather like philosophy of science, and it was modestly held that it was hardly within the province of a mere philosopher to teach the working scientist his business. Similarly the moralist's views were thought of as depending on experience of life, and on his feelings, good or otherwise, and the

Introduction

philosopher in his closet (or college) thought of himself as a relatively bloodless spectator. Not for him was the passion of the preacher or the moral reformer. Or if he did have such passions they were for his spare time, not for the professional activities for which he drew his salary. Why should the taxpayer pay him to propagate his private feelings about conduct, which might often be controversial and which might even be contrary to those of the said taxpayer? Scientists, of course, often come out with statements of fact that upset the taxpayer, but science was supposed to be an objectively assessable activity, in contrast to moralizing which was supposed to be subjective or an expression of the attitudes of the moralist, attitudes which need not be shared between rival moralists, so that these different moralists could only agree to differ (if they agreed even on that).

PROBLEMS ABOUT MEANING

Putting it a little crudely, the sort of analytic philosophy of which I am speaking saw itself as concerned with the meanings of moral words, such as 'ought', 'right', 'wrong', 'good' and 'bad'. It might be questioned, indeed, whether there is any such class of moral words, since these words are also used in non-moral contexts. The burglar may use the wrong jemmy, the mechanic ought to use a screwdriver, the grass in Canberra ought to be green by now, the batsman played a bad shot, but all the same he was facing a good bowler. So perhaps we should talk of the uses of these words in respectively moral and non-moral contexts. There then arises the question of how to define moral and non-moral contexts.[2] To do it in terms of contexts in which respectively moral and non-moral words were used would clearly bring us round in a circle.

Philosophers who talk of 'the moral words' have tended to try to get round this difficulty by distinguishing moral and non-moral senses of words, and to treat 'moral words' as signifying words used in moral, as opposed to non-moral, senses.

This view that words such as 'ought' and 'good' may have both moral and non-moral senses, so that each of them, in a way, can be thought of as two or more words, like 'bank' in 'river bank' and 'savings bank', is possibly a legacy to analytic philosophy

Introduction

from intuitionist theories. Philosophers such as G.E. Moore, H.A. Prichard and others held that moral principles were known by a faculty of intellectual intuition. This thesis is extremely implausible, since it is hard to see how a faculty of intellectual intuition, such as was postulated by Moore, could be reconcilable with a biological view of man, and it has other difficulties as well. Be this as it may, the theory implied a doctrine of moral and nonmoral senses, as Roger Wertheimer has pointed out,[3] since it would seem that no act of intellectual intuition is needed in order to know that this is the right screwdriver to use, that a batsman had played a good off-drive, or that the grass in Canberra ought to be green by now.

An enquiry into the meanings of the moral words is likely to rest heavily on a notion of 'meaning' which has been importantly criticized by W.V. Quine.[4] With this notion of meaning stands or falls the related notion of analyticity. An analytic sentence was supposed to express a true proposition solely in virtue of the meanings of the words in it. More precisely, a sentence was said to be analytic if it could be transformed into a sentence expressing a truth of logic purely by means of definitions and syntactical rules. There perhaps are analytic truths in this sense, but they are trivial and not of philosophical interest.[5] Thus, 'No bachelors are married' transforms into a truth of formal logic if we allow the definition of 'bachelor' as 'not married and not previously married adult man'. Even so there are problems about bachelors of arts, who need not be unmarried, and so it would need to be argued that there is an ambiguity in 'bachelor' here. (I am not saying that there is not.)

Quine's position is that there is in general no way of separating out what in language is made true by our linguistic conventions and what is made true by the facts of the world. I am guardedly happy about calling 'No bachelors are married' analytic because the notion of 'definition' seems applicable: there seems to be no harm in talking of a definition of bachelors as unmarried.[6] But in interesting cases, being definitional is a transitory characteristic of sentences. In other words, we take little or no notice of definitions when it suits us to ignore them. No doubt 'atom' was introduced *via* the definition 'indivisible particle of matter'. But no one (as far as I know) wanted to deny the epithet 'atom' to the entities in question when it was discovered that atoms were

Introduction

made up of protons and electrons (and later of neutrons). What is true is that at one time philosophers and scientists were strongly disposed to assent to the statement that atoms are indivisible and that at another time they were disposed strongly *not* to assent to it. In Sir Walter Scott's *Antiquary* (end of Chapter 37 and latter part of Chapter 38), set at the end of the eighteenth century, characters in the novel refer to seals as 'fish' and of the hunting of them as 'fishing'. Has the word 'fish' changed its meaning, or have we changed our beliefs about fish, for example that no fish are mammals? Has 'atom' changed its meaning likewise, or have we come to believe different things about atoms? I want to agree with Quine that these questions do not have much sense: what we can sensibly discuss is the changing pattern of assent and dissent to sentences containing 'atom' and 'fish' (though we can ask sensibly how well entrenched the sentences containing these words are in our theories: how much else we may be led to give up also if we give up these sentences).

Now if there is such a thing as 'the logic of the moral words', this so-called logic would have to be exhibited by means of analytic sentences containing the said words (not any analytic sentences, since the moral words might occur inessentially, as in 'If no unmarried men ought to sleep with a woman, then no bachelors ought to sleep with a woman'. Such a sentence is morally vacuous. Those who talk of the logic of words not special to formal logic would say that the above sentence was analytic in virtue of the logic of 'bachelor', not in virtue of the logic of 'ought'). If we are doubtful of analyticity, we will also be doubtful of the notion of a logic of the moral words.

The notions of meaning, synonymy and analyticity, and those of 'it not being a contradiction to say that', and of 'it being an open question that', have been deployed in discussions of the so-called 'naturalistic fallacy'. The term was introduced by G.E. Moore[7] though there have been earlier anticipations of the idea as by the eighteenth century writer Richard Price[8] and others.[9] Moore held that ethical concepts could not be defined in terms of those of natural science or metaphysics. Ethical words, he held, referred in some way to special 'non-natural' properties. The identification of ethical properties (for example, rightness) with natural ones (or with metaphysical ones) was in Moore's view

Introduction

the committing of a fallacy, which he called 'the naturalistic fallacy'.

In more recent philosophical literature, the term 'naturalistic fallacy' has been used in a slightly extended sense. Moore held that it was the fallacy of identifying ethical properties with non-ethical properties, and he held that statements of ethics, such as 'We ought not to cause avoidable misery', were statements of fact, but not of scientific or metaphysical fact. According to Moore these statements were about a special sort of ethical or 'non-natural' fact. More recently a 'non-cognitivist' view of ethics has been proposed, according to which ethical sentences do not express statements of fact, whether natural or non-natural, but rather express attitudes,[10] or make prescriptions, rather as imperative sentences do.[11] The naturalistic fallacy as so construed has been typically expressed by the slogan that 'ought' cannot be deduced from 'is'. On one interpretation this idea goes back to David Hume, in the last paragraph of the first section of Part 3 of Book I of his *Treatise of Human Nature*.

Non-naturalism, in this wider sense as well as in Moore's narrower one, has been defended by means of such arguments as that of 'the open question'. Thus it has been argued that whatever naturalistic definition of a moral concept is given, such as that 'right' means 'most conducive to the greatest general happiness', it is always an open question whether the proposition corresponding to the definition is true. Thus even if (as some would say) all and only right actions are those that conduce to the greatest general happiness, this is a substantive assertion which can meaningfully be questioned. If there were a contradiction in saying that a right action does not conduce to the general happiness then the assertion that right action conduces to the general happiness would be a trivial and uninteresting one, not the exciting moral principle that its proponents presumably believe it to be. 'Right actions conduce to the general happiness' cannot, so the argument goes, be an analytic sentence.

I want to defend the view that there is something correct about such arguments that 'ought' (and 'right' and 'good') cannot be derived from 'is'. Nevertheless they rely heavily on such notions as 'meaning' (as in 'it is not part of the *meaning* of "right" that right actions conduce to the general happiness'), analyticity, definition, and so on, which following Quine I wish to eschew,

Introduction

except occasionally, as in Chapter 2, for the sake of argument against those who *do* use the notions.

META-ETHICS AND NORMATIVE ETHICS

The statement that 'ought' cannot be deduced from 'is' seems to be one of those statements that are 'second order' – statements *about* moral discourse, not statements *within* moral discourse. The distinction has sometimes been made in terms of the distinction between 'meta-ethics' and 'normative ethics'. Normative ethics is the putting forward of a more or less systematic corpus of moral recommendations. Kant's philosophy of the categorical imperative, Sidgwick's utilitarianism, Rawls's theory of justice, and on a less systematic level the ten commandments and the beatitudes, all contain or imply first order ethical recommendations. Meta-ethics was supposed to do no such thing. It was supposed to be neutral with respect to normative ethics. It was thought of, perhaps, as analogous to meta-mathematics, or proof theory in mathematics. However, meta-mathematics can be given a precise definition in a way that meta-ethics cannot. Of course, the English word 'meta' is pretty vague. The classical Greek word has the meaning of 'after'. Metaphysics was so called because it investigates the sorts of questions discussed in Aristotle's *Metaphysics*, which in turn was so-called because it came after his *Physics*. There is no suggestion of 'second order' here. But the words 'meta-ethics' and 'normative ethics' are quite useful as suggesting the sort of supposed distinction between 'second order' and 'first order' questions with which I have been concerned in this chapter.

It should be conceded that the distinction is not a clear one, and it may in the end have to be abandoned, though clearly some ethical statements will always be felt to be at the normative end of this spectrum, and others at the meta-ethical end. Roughly, the less an ethical statement has implications for practice the more it will tend to the meta-ethical end of the spectrum. The fact that a sentence is second order, in that it mentions or refers to other sentences, does not in itself make it meta-ethical. Thus, if I say that some moral statements are true or correct, I am making a second order statement which disquotationally implies

Introduction

these moral statements themselves, and so is as normative as can be. Roger N. Hancock has pointed out[12] that the second order statement 'It is wrong to make general statements in ethics' is itself a quite clearly normative statement. Hancock also considers biographical statements to the effect that someone uttered an ethical statement, and points out that though these are second order and also ethically neutral, they are not of the sort that would commonly be regarded as part of meta-ethics. This is perhaps because they are insufficiently general or theoretical.

Statements that seem at first sight to be ethically neutral and part of the analysis of meanings can be in fact normative and questionable from a normative point of view. Thus if we were to characterize morality as a set of moral prescriptions in which the interests of all are treated equally we would rule out particular egoism, and it seems to be essentialism to rule out egoism from being a morality. (By 'particular egoism' I mean the view expressed by someone who says 'I ought to look after my own interests exclusively', not the universal egoism which would be expressed by someone who said 'Everyone ought to look after his or her interests exclusively'.) Particular egoism is at any rate a principle on which someone might decide to plan his or her life (whether regrettably or otherwise). If we are suspicious of analyticity we will be suspicious of any such way of getting a normative rabbit out of an analytic hat. It also seems to me to be essentialist to characterize morality by its content, as has been done by G.J. Warnock[13] and Philippa Foot.[14] Philippa Foot has held that 'Clasp your hands three times every hour' could not be a *moral* principle. But if one is not essentialist about morality one may want to say that such a principle could be a moral one, though of course a very silly one.

R.M. Hare has over many years developed a very interesting theory of ethics which has resulted in a form of utilitarianism.[15] He gives what he takes to be a purely formal characterization of morality. (1) An ethical statement is *prescriptive*. Roughly, if I sincerely assert an ethical statement of the form 'I ought to do X', I also am disposed to comply with the imperative 'Do X'. (2) An ethical statement (or prescription) is universalizable. If we accept it we must accept a related statement which is universal in form and contains no proper name or indexical expression or any other reference to a specific individual or group of individuals or

Introduction

particular place or time. For example, if Bill Sikes were to hold that, in circumstances C, he ought to steal Tom Jones's money, then (consistently with the meaning of the word 'ought') he must hold that anyone just like him (in circumstances C) ought to steal from someone just like Tom Jones. One must imaginatively put oneself in other people's shoes (and in the paws, fins, etc. of other sentient creatures?[16]) and this involves imagining that we have *their* preferences not ours.[17] (If I had a violin I would not mind Bill Sikes stealing it, since I can't play the violin, but I would mind him stealing my squash racquet.) (3) Moral prescriptions are over-riding. Thus it may be aesthetically right to do something but morally wrong, and if I accept the moral prescription I must in such a case refuse to accept the aesthetic one.[18] Or if I did allow an ostensibly aesthetic and universal preference to over-ride an ostensibly moral and universal one, the ostensibly aesthetic preference would be a moral one.

What these requirements demand is that we treat the preferences of other sentient beings as if they were our own.[19] I shall not go through the steps in Hare's argument that this equal treatment of preferences of others follows from acceptance of the three formal requirements. A thorough discussion of Hare's subtle book would require a separate work. I wish merely to point out that Hare claims to show how a particular set of moral recommendations are determined by (a) the above-mentioned formal characteristics of the moral concepts, and (b) empirical data about the preferences of sentient beings. His system is a broadly utilitarian one with which I have considerable sympathy. My query is as to whether it is uniquely determined by Hare's starting point. How would it decide between (a) a principle of simply maximizing total preference-satisfaction and (b) of modifying the maximization by some principle of fair distribution of satisfaction of preference? Or what about some system of a neo-Kantian sort, such as at present is being worked out by my colleague Stanley Benn, in which the leading idea is 'respect for persons'? Hare's answer is that such non-utilitarian systems are dependent on special intuitions (I would say 'preferences') of the proposers of such systems, and not by the requirements of universalizability, prescriptivity and full factual information. Hare's requirements for a moral theory are therefore rather strong, since other systems that are in some sense prescriptive and universal, such as those that modify utilitarianism by a principle of fair distribution, or those that are based on a respect for persons, have a claim to be regarded as 'moral'.

I am indeed not sure how much Hare need disagree with these remarks. He talks of his constraints leading to clear-headed people *in practice*[20] coming to agree to the same evaluation (my italics). He also agrees[21] that to treat 'moral' as (approximately) equivalent to 'over-riding-prescriptive-universalizable' is in some sort a proposal, and so he perhaps avoids any worries about essentialism in the definition of morality.

D.H. Monro[22] has characterized morality in terms of prescription in accordance with one's highest order desires, over-riding attitudes in a sense of 'over-riding' perhaps not quite the same as Hare's, but related to it. One desire will be higher than another in the hierarchy of a person's desires if it is in part a disposition to act in ways so as to strengthen or weaken the lower order desire. An attitude (or attitudes) which is (or are) highest in the hierarchy are what are expressed by our ultimate moral principles. In this sense particular egoism can be a moral principle, even though it is ruled out as such by Hare's criteria. Now certainly egoism is one option when someone is considering various plans of life. We might wish for something else, such as a principle of universal benevolence, but surely it is one option to be considered. (And as Bishop Butler contended, enlightened self-interest is on the whole much less dangerous to others than are many other common springs of action.[23]) Indeed a *powerful* egoist might not mind other people having this plan of life too. To this extent he might be prepared to universalize. He would not worry about the possibility that *if* he were in the other's position he would not like it. He would not worry (as urged to do by Hare) about what would be his feelings in a merely *possible* world in which he was in the other's shoes.[24] He would be prepared to universalize but only for the actual world (or possible worlds that branch off at the time of decision from the actual world), where he knows that he is top dog. A less powerful egoist would not be happy to universalize even this much. He would make his plan of life on egoistic grounds, but would conceal his egoism from others.

Moral discourse, as we find it in real life, is unfortunately a far cry from the more or less lucid combination of prescriptions and factual considerations that we find in the writings of philosophers. To give a philosophical analysis and critique of real-life moral discourse, such as we find in newspaper editorials, sermons, or in private conversations, would be a messy business. For example, practical morality has been, especially in past centuries, almost inextricably intertwined with religion and theology. Consider the case of Jeanie Deans, in Sir Walter Scott's great novel, *The Heart of Midlothian*.[25] She is a young woman of great character and heroism, very affectionate and much imbued with the stern religious precepts of her Cameronian father. Her younger sister Effie is tried on a technical charge of child murder. There is no proof of the death of the child, but, under the draconian law of the time, concealment of pregnancy is taken as proof of murder. If Jeanie will only tell the court that Effie had told her of the pregnancy then Effie will be acquitted, but Jeanie refuses to perjure herself and Effie is sentenced to death. Subsequently Jeanie travels, mostly on foot, to London, and successfully pleads with the Queen for a pardon. For Effie she will sacrifice 'everything but truth and conscience'. But if we try to disentangle what the motives of conscience in fact were, we can think of many different things. There is the reluctance to break a rule that she had been taught as a child. There is the reluctance to upset her father (who would be even more upset by the breaking of a Biblical commandment than by the shame and death of his younger daughter – to modern eyes he is not an entirely admirable character). There is the fact that the precept against telling lies is a Divine commandment, and so fear of God and also of hell fire comes into it very strongly. There is the complication that the fear of God is a mixture of awe for the numinous and fear in the sense of 'being frightened'. All these things are entangled together. Would Jeanie have told her white lie if she had gone to university to study philosophy and had been argued into atheism or at least a more liberal theism?

It is clear that the picture of ethics as depending on (a) universal prescriptions and (b) empirically ascertainable facts is too simple. Metaphysical argument is often relevant to ethical disputes. I would put it on the 'fact' side of the usual 'fact-value' distinction, but it complicates issues in a different way. The way in which traditionally morals and religion have been mixed up with each other also makes it perhaps impossible to disentangle,

Introduction

in cases such as that of Jeanie Deans, those attitudes that a fastidious Oxford philosopher would allow as 'moral' from those that are prudential or religious. A similar messy situation seems to me to exist today in popular and ecclesiastical discussions about the morality or otherwise of abortion. There is also a great admixture of rhetoric in popular moral discourse, and much use of perhaps dubious analogies. To make a comprehensive study of some real-life moral disputes would take us far afield from the traditional concerns of meta-ethics.

MEANING AND TRUTH

If, following Quine, and as I have suggested earlier that we should do, we try to eschew the notion of meaning, is there anything useful with which we can replace it? There is of course *paraphrase*: we may try to replace some sentence by a more perspicuous one, utterance of which would suit certain purposes of the speaker, as well as would the utterance of the original sentence. However, this is a matter of the pragmatics of language (with which I shall indeed be concerned in a later chapter), rather than with semantics (roughly the theory of meaning, truth and denotation).

What about truth and denotation? We have certain paradigms which could not be more perspicuous. We have Alfred Tarski's paradigm, exemplified by ' "Snow is white" is true if and only if snow is white', ' ". . . loves . . ." is true of an ordered pair of items if and only if the first loves the second', and ' "Ann" denotes Ann'. (In the sort of canonical notation desired by Quine we would not have the last of these, because the name 'Ann' would be eliminated in favour of the expression 'The x such that x anns', where for something to ann would be to have whatever set of predicates are true of it and single out Ann.) Donald Davidson refers to sentences of the form ' "Snow is white" is true if and only if snow is white' as 'T-sentences'.

These paradigms look so trivial that it is easy to fail to see the point of Tarski's theory of truth. After all, any T-sentence follows trivially from the axiom schema '$\ulcorner p \urcorner$ is true if and only if p'.[26] Nevertheless it should be noted that this axiom schema constitutes an *infinite* number of axioms. (There are infinitely

Introduction

many ways of replacing the letter '*p*' in it by a sentence.) Tarski's achievement was to show how all the infinite number of T-sentences of a language formalized within first order predicate logic could be deduced from a *finite* number of axioms that give truth conditions for the connectives such as 'not' and 'or', for the quantifiers 'all' and 'some', and for the primitive predicates of the language – saying what objects (or sequences of objects) these predicates are 'true of' (or 'satisfied by'). (I omit here a minor technical complication.) Tarski's theory gives a recursive account of what it is for any sentence of a language that is expressible in first order predicate logic to be true, so that if, let us suppose, some horribly long and complicated sentence covered two big blackboards, Tarski's theory would tell us what it was for such a sentence to be true, provided we knew the finite set of truth conditions for the constituents. Admittedly these last look trivial, for example that the disjunction of two sentences is true if and only if one or the other is true, but what is not trivial is the recursiveness of the whole theory.

Tarski's theory has important applications for the philosophy of mathematics. Kurt Gödel showed that in any axiomatic system as strong as elementary number theory there will be a sentence neither provable nor disprovable from the axioms but which is nevertheless true. Tarski's theory gave a clear account of truth in mathematics which was needed since mathematical truth could no longer be regarded as provability. Indeed, semantical theories, such as Donald Davidson's,[27] make it quite clear, as I think any acceptable semantic theory should, that truth cannot be identified with any such notion as provability, verifiability, or warranted assertibility. Certainly Michael Dummett and others have tried to restore a connection between truth and warranted assertibility, but the present book is no place to go into these controversies. In so far as what is said in this book is taken to presuppose some semantic theory, it should be taken to propose some semantic theory akin to that of Davidson, even though I can remain open-minded about the exact form it will take. It need not, for example, be based only on first order logic, if it turns out that devices are needed that are not found in first order logic, provided that certain conditions are met, the chief one being that the theory still gives a recursive account of the truth conditions for the language. For imperative sentences we shall need to talk of compliance rather than of truth, but a theory of compliance conditions can be made parasitic on a theory of truth conditions.

A Davidsonian truth theory for a language should enable us to deduce all T-sentences of the language. Thus ' "Snow is white" is true if and only if snow is white' should be deducible from the finite set of axioms of the theory. But can this be a theory of 'meaning' for the language? Since the 'if and only if' is extensional, it follows that $\ulcorner\ulcorner p \urcorner$ is true if and only if $q \urcorner$ is true if and only if $\ulcorner p \urcorner$ and $\ulcorner q \urcorner$ have the same truth value. It may therefore be objected that on this theory ' "Snow is white" is true if and only if grass is green' could equally 'give the meaning'. The reply is that it is not just the T-sentences that 'give the meaning' but the way they are proved from the axioms. It is not plausible that ' "Snow is white" is true if and only if grass is green' could be proved from a finitely axiomatized T-theory. The notion of meaning is still not the strong but suspect notion of ordinary philosophical discourse about meanings. Nevertheless the requirement of provability of a T-sentence makes it stronger than that of mere extensional equivalence. Here I have been assuming that the T-theory and the language it is a theory of are both (say) English. But we might have a T-theory for French in which a T-sentence might be ' "La neige est blanche" is true if and only if snow is white'. A T-theory of a foreign language will illustrate further features of a T-theory. This is clear when we consider the case of devising a T-theory for a quite exotic language, for which we do not have any philological clues, as exist in the case of French. This is the situation of 'radical interpretation' and T-sentences have to be conjectured on empirical evidence. Then the T-theory is tested by its ability to yield the T-sentences. This gives the notion of 'meaning' as elucidated by T-theories a certain holistic character. This will be further explained in the next chapter, where I shall try to use the notion of radical interpretation to shed light on various meta-ethical theories.

IMPERATIVES AND COMPLIANCE

Sometimes moralists use not the indicative with 'ought' but simply the imperative. Instead of 'You ought to honour your

Introduction

father and mother' we have 'Honour your father and mother'. Besides imperatives like the just-mentioned one, that are signified as imperative by the inflection and the position of the main verb of a sentence, there are others which are of the form 'Let it be the case that p' where 'p' is a dummy for a sentence in the indicative mood. In colloquial language such sentences are usually contracted. 'Let it be the case that everyone marries someone' is replaced by 'Let everyone marry someone'. How should we deal with the semantics of imperatives? Since an utterance of an imperative is neither true nor false how does the semantics of sentences in the imperative mood relate to a truth theory? Tarski's theory of truth was designed for a language appropriate to mathematics or theoretical science, in which indexical and contextual elements have been eliminated, or are unimportant. (Contextual elements cannot be eliminated *entirely* – consider the satisfaction condition for 'x is a field' as it occurs in a book of algebra and in a book of electro-magnetism, respectively, not to mention how it occurs in a book of agriculture!) For natural languages with indexical elements, such as 'I', 'you', 'now', 'here', and the tenses, the notions of satisfaction and of truth have to be relativized to a person and a time. 'You will come' is true relative to person P at t if and only if the person addressed by P at t comes later than t (where 'comes' is tenseless).[28]

The semantics of imperatives is a still more controversial subject than that of indicatives. I propose to follow those who have taken 'compliance' to be the imperative analogue of truth. Thus just as 'I will shut the window or open the door' is true when said by Jones at midday on 1st April 1982 if 'I will shut the window' is true as said by Jones at midday on 1st April 1982, so 'Shut the door or open the window' as said by Jones at midday is complied with if 'Shut the door' said by Jones at midday is complied with. 'Complied with' should here be understood as 'complied with by the addressee of the utterance of the imperative'. (In the case of third person imperatives the case is different. The Colonel says to the Adjutant '[Let it be the case that] the battalion moves at 0600 hours'. This is addressed to the Adjutant, but complied with by the battalion as a whole, or perhaps the officer in the leading vehicle.) Sometimes an utterance of an imperative will have many addressees: indeed

Introduction

imperatives can be quite general, like 'Honour your father and mother'. Here 'complied with' can be taken as 'complied with by a particular selected addressee' or as 'complied with by all addressees'. Often it will not matter which interpretation is adopted. To simplify the exposition in what follows I shall often omit the clauses required to deal with indexicals, since they can easily be supplied mentally by the reader.

Let us write 'You honour your father and mother' as 'It is the case that you honour your father and mother', and let us write 'Honour your father and mother' as 'Let it be the case that you honour your father and mother'. We can now write a dummy indicative sentence as 'Ap', where 'A' corresponds to 'It is the case that', and we can write a dummy imperative sentence as 'Ip', where 'I' corresponds to 'Let it be the case that'.

In classical truth functional logic we say that A(pvq) follows from Ap which in turn follows from A$(p.q)$. That is if Ap is true so must A(pvq) be true, and Ap must be true if A$(p.q)$ is true. Similarly we can say that I(pvq) follows from Ip and Ip follows from I$(p.q)$. If Ip is complied with so must I(pvq) be complied with, and Ip must be complied with if I$(p.q)$ is complied with. Similarly A$(\sim p)$ is true if Ap is false (*i.e.* not true) and I$(\sim p)$ is complied with if Ip is not complied with. In the above 'must be' should be read as referring to all models, or all assignments of truth values (or compliance values) to the letters 'p' and 'q'.

In practice we are interested not only in deducing imperatives from other imperatives but in deducing imperatives from premises some of which are indicative and others of which are imperative. We also use mixed sentences, such as 'If Smith comes telephone me'. We can say that 'If Smith comes telephone me' is complied with if and only if either Smith comes and the addressee telephones the utterer or else Smith doesn't come (and the addressee does anything whatever).

I am inclined to think that mixtures of imperatives occur in colloquial language only in the form A$p \supset$ Iq (and perhaps in a rather strained way in the form ApvIq which comes to the same as A$(\sim p) \supset$ Iq.[29] We do not get Ap.Iq though we do get Ap and Iq asserted as separate premises. I do not think we ever get I$p \supset$ Aq, even though this would be a way of saying A$(\sim q) \supset$ I$(\sim p)$.

Introduction

We can now consider arguments with both indicative and imperative premisses. We can reduce these to the form in which there is one indicative premiss and one imperative premiss, because we can form the conjunctions of all the indicative and imperative premisses respectively. We need consider only arguments with an imperative conclusion, since arguments with an indicative conclusion do not normally occur. (This is connected with the fact that we do not get in colloquial language such forms as $Ip \supset Iq$, though we do get, in *almost* colloquial discourse, $Ip \therefore Iq$.)

Then an argument $Ap.Iq \therefore Ir$ is valid if under every re-interpretation of the sentences here represented by the dummies 'p', 'q' and 'r', whenever Ap is true and Iq is complied with, Ir is complied with. These sentences may contain quantifiers as in the argument: 'All rabbits are mammals, get me a rabbit, so get me a mammal'.

Because of the quantifiers 'all' and 'some' a semantics for imperatives cannot rely merely on compliance conditions. Compliance is the analogue of truth, a predicate being 'true of' an object, or more generally of satisfaction of an open sentence by a sequence, e.g. 'x is between y and z' being satisfied by the sequence <York, London, Edinburgh>. So the semantics of imperatives will have to be parasitic on the semantics of indicatives, which has to be based on the notion of satisfaction, rather than truth, because of the quantifiers. That is, the internal quantificational semantics of the sentences that go after the 'It is the case that' or 'Let it be the case that' will be given in the normal Tarski method. Indeed this parasitic method could have been given for the internal truth functional structure, as in sentences of the form $I(pvq)$, for example, but it may be more instructive to use the direct approach of compliance conditions, as I have done in previous paragraphs.

Some philosophers have worried about the legitimacy of inferences from Ip to $I(pvq)$ or from IFa to $I(\exists x)Fx$. If I tell you to give the patient a drink of orange juice, and you deduce the command 'Give the patient orange juice or methylated spirits', you may, it is said, comply with the latter command by giving the patient methylated spirits (and so killing him). Similarly if I tell you to give the patient something to drink, you may deduce the command to give the patient methylated spirits to drink, comply

Introduction

with this command, and kill the patient. But if you do this you forget the definition of implication in terms of compliance conditions. To comply with the premiss is to comply with the conclusion, but not *vice versa*. Similarly for the indicative 'John met Mary' to be true is for a legitimate conclusion 'John met Mary or Ann' to be true, but not *vice versa*. It is admittedly *misleading* to say 'John met Mary or Ann' when you know that the person in question met Mary, but it is not *false*. It is a breach of a conversational implicature (in H.P. Grice's sense[30]). That is, it breaches the convention that one does not make a weaker statement when one is in a position to make a stronger one. Similarly to utter the imperative 'Shut the door or shoot the secretary', when what you want obeyed is the stronger imperative 'Shut the door', or to utter the command 'Appoint someone' when what you want obeyed is the stronger command 'Appoint Mary', would be a breach of a similar convention. Such breaches of convention can be dangerous, and when not dangerous they can be pointless. But this has to do with the pragmatics of language, not its semantics. To utter certain conclusions that have been deduced from stronger premisses (whether indicative or imperative) can be pointless or dangerous, but these conclusions are conclusions none the less.[31]

Consider, again, the case of a man who utters two imperatives that together imply a contradiction. Consider in particular the simple case of $Ip.I(\sim p)$ (or $I(p.\sim p)$). From this we can deduce Ir, for arbitrary r. Thus from 'Shut the door and do not shut the door' we could deduce 'Rob the bank'.

It may be objected that from the fact that someone utters contradictory imperatives nothing follows for action. This is correct but no objection. 'Someone uttered contradictory imperatives' is an indicative not an imperative. From 'Shut the door and do not shut the door' the imperative 'Rob the bank' does indeed follow. To say it follows is to say that one cannot comply with the premisses without complying with the conclusion. This is indeed so in the present example, simply because one cannot comply with the premisses. The right attitude on the part of the recipient of the contradictory imperatives would be to say that since, whatever the recipient does, he or she will disobey one of these imperatives, he or she might as well disobey the conclusion too. The recipient could add that someone who uttered contradictory imperatives must be an unreliable source of practical advice, and so there would be no motive for trying to comply with the other's imperatives.

This brief look at the semantics of indicatives and imperatives is based on a Tarskian approach. There is some controversy about how far this can be extended to cover all the semantics of ordinary language, as is the goal of Donald Davidson's research programme. One extension would be to extend talk of the actual world to talk of possible worlds other than the actual world. Because in ethics we consider alternative possibilities of action I shall make a minimal and I hope harmless use of this extension (harmless to the extent that I shall use an interpretation of possible worlds that makes them part of the actual world). This will make for simplicity of exposition. I am not sure that it is necessary. Howard Burdick has produced an ingenious theory,[32] in the spirit of W.V. Quine and Donald Davidson, but with significant differences, in which he has given an extensional theory of the propositional attitudes, e.g. for contexts of the forms 'Smith believes that *p*' and 'Smith desires that *p*' which had provided difficulty for Davidson, even though Davidson had made some attempt to deal with them.[33] Burdick's approach may well have far reaching effects on the philosophy of language.

Unlike 'Let everyone honour his or her father or mother', the sentence 'Everyone ought to honour his or her father or mother' is an indicative one, even though *pragmatically* it may be used so as to function like an imperative sentence. Something will be said about the semantics of 'ought' sentences in Chapter 4.

'MORAL' AND 'ETHICAL'

At the beginning of this chapter I introduced the distinction (so far as there is one) between meta-ethics and normative ethics. The term 'moral philosophy' is generally used to cover both of these fields. The etymology of 'moral' connects it with Latin 'mos' for 'custom', whose plural is 'mores', and we still talk of the mores of a society. The etymology thus suggests anthropology or sociology rather than what today would usually be called 'moral philosophy'. The etymology of 'ethics' is more complex. It is derived from the Greek 'ēthos' (long 'ē') meaning 'character', but

Introduction

there is also in Greek 'ethos' (short 'e') meaning 'custom'. Aristotle in his *Nichomachean Ethics*, 1103 *a* 17, talks of the latter as a variation on the former. Whether this is so or not, there is an easy transition from the thought of the customary behaviour of an individual and hence of his dispositions, including his virtues and vices, to that of the customs of a society. This also indicates how we get the use of 'moral' as in 'the moral sciences', which at Cambridge University covered not only philosophy in general, as well as moral philosophy in particular, but also psychology and at one time economics. The inclusion of psychology also comes from a certain confusion of thought, where it was supposed that the sort of investigations typically done by philosophers were somehow about the mind: Hume thought that his *Treatise* was an essay about the mental realm that corresponded to Newton's treatises about the physical world. Sometimes in Britain and elsewhere this confusion was perpetuated when 'mental philosophy' was contrasted with 'natural philosophy', that is, with physics.

'Moral' is therefore a more protean word than 'ethics'. It even intrudes into talk of probability, as in 'It is a moral certainty'. On the other hand, among moral philosophers the word 'moral' has had a narrower application, and has even lost much of its connection with the notion of custom or mores, since moral philosophers have been concerned much more with the individual conscience which can go contrary to the mores of society.

In the light of my earlier rejection of any appeal to analyticity, and as I have indicated earlier, I naturally also want to reject any notion that morality has an essence. Appreciation of the protean and imprecise character of the word 'moral' merely increases this desire, and makes one a bit careful about putting much philosophical weight on phrases such as 'the point of view of morality' or 'the purpose of morality'. Of course, one may ask about the purpose of a system of conventions in a quasi-Darwinian way, somewhat as a physiologist may talk of the purpose or function of a certain neural structure.[34] The theory of evolution by natural selection makes it a good bet that a given physiological structure is *as if* it were designed, even though the theory also implies that it *is not* designed. The purpose is an 'as if' purpose – it is as if the structure was designed to promote survival of the species. Often of course it is not as if it was

Introduction

designed. The human sinus is as if it were badly designed, since the drainage hole is at the top not the bottom. The theory of evolution also explains this appearance of bad design too, because we have evolved from four-footed animals whose heads hung downwards. In the same way a set of rules or customs in a society may have evolved as a result of unplanned co-ordinations by members of the society, or in some other way, as by the actions of some sort of leader or prophet, and have been retained because the society functioned well in its environment or in competition with other societies. But when we look at morality as it exists in the decisions of the individual conscience this notion of a purpose of morality loses even this quasi-Darwinian and 'as if' force. The individual who decides does have his purposes, but these are not the purposes of something called 'morality'.

Does moral language (if there is such a separately specifiable part of language) have a function? Could we do without the language of 'ought', whether in moral or non-moral contexts? These questions are concerned not with the semantics of moral language but with its pragmatics. I shall be concerned with this issue in Chapter 3, where a certain paradox will be considered, a paradox that arises from the idea that we primarily make use of distinctively moral language in order to persuade others. But to prepare the way for Chapter 3 I wish temporarily to revert to a more traditional way of looking at matters, and to consider the question of the so-called naturalistic fallacy, assuming for the sake of argument, at the outset, that there are moral senses of 'ought' and 'good'. This assumption will be reconsidered later.

II
INTERLUDE ON THE NATURALISTIC FALLACY

MOORE AND THE NATURALISTIC FALLACY

In this chapter I shall discuss the question of the so-called naturalistic fallacy, which has played such a central role in contemporary meta-ethics. Because I want to put my own position into the context of some of the traditional approaches I shall for the sake of argument begin by temporarily absolving myself from my resolution to avoid notions like that of 'meaning' and 'analyticity', or at any rate to use them very sparingly, and will concede for the moment that there are specifically ethical senses of words such as 'good' and 'right'.

The term 'naturalistic fallacy' was introduced by G.E. Moore, and it can be questioned whether it is either naturalistic or a fallacy. Nevertheless, I have a strong propensity to argue that there is something very right about Moore's position, though it is hard to state it clearly. My own youthful introduction to ethics was through reading Moore's *Principia Ethica*. For a time, as an undergraduate, I was spoiled for ethics because I could not see anything much wrong with Moore's book. The generation of today may well be surprised at this, because of course, as I soon came to see, there is much wrong with it (though I have never ceased to be attracted by Moore's consequentialism in normative ethics). By modern standards Moore's philosophy of language is hopelessly confused, and so is his moral epistemology. Moore's philosophy was Platonistic in that he believed in a realm of

Interlude on the naturalistic fallacy

ethical and other characteristics, of which the central one was intrinsic goodness, which was discovered by intellectual intuition. This intellectual intuition enabled us to make synthetic *a priori* judgments that whatever had certain more mundane characteristics, for example, pleasantness, had also, at least *pro tanto*, the non-natural characteristic of goodness.

Now various philosophers will have various objections to Moore's epistemology here. Here I wish only to point out how hard it is to reconcile it with a biological view of the human mind, remembering that modern biology is extremely mechanistic. There is no room in such a view for intellectual intuition of Moore's Platonistic sort. We can see how natural selection might enable a more complex neural structure to develop, how a mutation might lead to a different twist in the anatomy of the brain, but how could it lead to a totally immaterial faculty of intellectual intuition?

Nevertheless, with all its obscurities and implausibilities *Principia Ethica* still seems to me to be an important and powerful book. Even when it is obscure or when conclusions do not follow from premisses Moore still often has his eye on something philosophically important. In particular this is so with Moore's discussion of what he called 'the naturalistic fallacy'.

According to Moore the naturalistic fallacy is that of defining an ethical characteristic (in particular, that of goodness) in terms of non-ethical characteristics. He called it 'the naturalistic fallacy' because the commonest cases of such an alleged fallacy were cases in which 'good' (in what he took to be a specifically ethical sense of this word) was defined by means of common-sense psychological characteristics, such as pleasantness, or in terms of the notions of some scientific theory, such as the theory of evolution, when 'good' might be defined in such terms as 'conduciveness to survival'. But as his chapter on metaphysical ethics indicates, he also regarded metaphysical definitions of goodness, such as 'being united with a supersensible reality' as committing the naturalistic fallacy. W.K. Frankena, in his influential paper 'The naturalistic fallacy', claimed that the fallacy (or mistake) that Moore had obscurely in mind was a species of what Frankena called 'the definist fallacy'.[1] This is the mistake of identifying two distinct properties, that is, of defining one predicate by means of another predicate in terms of which the

Interlude on the naturalistic fallacy

first predicate cannot be defined. But if 'bachelor' can be defined as 'never married adult male' there is (tautologically) no mistake in defining 'bachelor' in such a way. Could it not be like this with a definition of 'good'? In this way, according to Frankena, Moore begs the question against the naturalist. To define 'good' as 'pleasant' (say) would be a mistake only if 'good' cannot be defined as 'pleasant'. And this is the very point at issue.

Moore contended that whatever naturalistic definition of 'good' is proposed, it is always an *open question* whether what possesses the characteristic referred to in the definition is good. As Frankena points out, this is once more the very question at issue, since the naturalist who holds that 'good' means 'pleasant' (say) will deny that there is an open question here, in the present case as to whether pleasure is good. Moore also held that 'good' stands for a *simple* property, and so could not be defined in terms of some *other* property, simple or complex. Once more this is to beg the question as to whether 'good' and 'pleasant' (say) stand for the same property. Moreover a non-naturalist might hold, as A.C. Ewing did, that 'good' could be defined in terms of some other ethical word, such as 'ought', and so the alleged simplicity or otherwise of goodness is not a vital issue for the non-naturalist.[2]

Frankena rightly contends, therefore, that the naturalistic fallacy, as conceived by Moore, is not a fallacy in anything like the logician's sense of that word. It is at worst merely a mistake, and whether a particular supposed case of it is a mistake or not cannot be settled by general rules, as a fallacy in logic can, but only by examining the particular case in question, and investigating whether it is or is not an open question whether something which answers to the definition is or is not good.

When Moore said that 'good' does not refer to any 'natural' property, perhaps he ought to have said that it does not refer to a property at all. (I do not like this talk of predicates referring to properties, since predicates are not names or referring expressions at all, but it is necessary if we are to discuss Moore without circumlocution. We cannot discuss everything at once and so let us continue to go along with his crude semantics for a bit.) As is well known, emotive and imperativist theories of ethics (non-cognitivist theories) have detached Moore's 'non-naturalism' from his intuitionism, and have tried to explain the difference

Interlude on the naturalistic fallacy

between ethical and non-ethical language in a way that is consistent with a naturalistic view of the human mind. After all 'non-natural' as used by Moore smacks rather of 'supernatural'. Non-cognitivists hold that when Moore said that 'good' does not stand for a non-natural property, what he should have said is rather that it does not stand for a property at all. According to non-cognitivists ethical utterances do not make statements at all, ethical or otherwise (or in so far as they make statements these are not distinctively ethical); they express ethical feelings or make prescriptions, as utterances of imperatives might.

Non-cognitivists support their theories in the same way as that in which Moore supported his, namely by contending that no naturalistic definitions of 'good', 'ought', 'right' and so on will do because it is always an open question whether something which is good, say, possesses certain naturalistic properties. In which case to brand a professed definition as a case of the naturalistic fallacy is still a case of *petitio principii*. Nevertheless, the non-cognitivist has another line of argument open to him which was not open to Moore. This is to relate the alleged contrast between ethical and factual language to the difference between desire and belief. The intuitionist has to explain the apparent connection between admitting that something is good and having at least some desire for it by reference to an *ad hoc* principle, namely that as a matter of fact we desire what we believe has the non-natural property of goodness. If the intuitionist were right there would be nothing paradoxical in someone being convinced that he ought to do something and saying that this gave him a very good reason for doing the opposite. The connection between goodness or rightness and desire would be analogous to that between sweetness of sugar and desire: some people like sugar in their tea and some do not, and some people might like goodness or rightness and others detest it. If this seems paradoxical, non-cognitivism gains in attractiveness.

Considerations such as these make it natural to relate the so-called naturalistic fallacy to the fallacy of deducing 'ought' from 'is'. Moore's naturalistic fallacy is not a fallacy in the logical sense, that is, deduction of a conclusion from premises that do not imply it. Moore's theory implies that one cannot validly deduce 'ought' purely from 'is', but he describes the naturalistic fallacy in less general terms. If we wish to detach what is good in

Interlude on the naturalistic fallacy

Moore from his intuitionism, it is natural to say that what Moore was *really* getting at is the impossibility of deducing 'ought' from 'is', and to see a celebrated statement by David Hume (*Treatise* III-1-1, final paragraph) as an anticipation of Moore. It is hard to be sure whether Hume is best interpreted as a non-cognitivist or as a subjectivist, but at any rate he brings out the connection between ethics and desire in a way that Moore did not.

'OUGHT' AND 'IS'

Thus it is natural to think of the naturalistic fallacy as the fallacy of deducing ethical precepts from non-ethical (e.g. scientific) statements of fact. This is clearly analogous to the fallacy (if it is a fallacy) of deducing imperatives from indicatives. But is it a fallacy to deduce imperatives from indicatives? Consider the indicative 'Greg Chappell is the most elegant batsman in Australia'. If imperatives can be joined by 'if . . . then . . .', as in Hare's *Language of Morals*,[3] Chapter 3, we can construct the imperative in hypothetical form (not to be confused with Kant's 'hypothetical imperatives'): 'If go to watch the most elegant batsman in Australia then go to watch Greg Chappell'. If the doctrine that imperatives cannot be deduced from indicatives is to be acceptable we must find some way of ruling out such cases, just as if the doctrine that 'ought' cannot be deduced from 'is' is to be made acceptable we must find a way of ruling out deductions such as that of 'If you ought to watch the most elegant batsman in Australia then you ought to watch Greg Chappell' from the premiss 'Greg Chappell is the most elegant batsman in Australia'.

If we define an ethical sentence as one that contains some expression from an ethical vocabulary, we have the problem of delimiting the ethical vocabulary. Let us for the moment suppose that this is done by some enumeration of words. (Since the number of words in any vocabulary is finite this enumeration will be a finite one.) Among the enumerated words will of course be the word 'ought'. We will also construe 'word' here so that a word used in two different senses counts as two words, and make use of the assumption, which was made purely for the sake of argument, that we can distinguish moral senses of words. If we define an ethical sentence as one containing at least one ethical word, it is clear that we can indeed deduce an ethical sentence from a set of non-ethical premisses. Obviously, by the above definition, if q is an ethical sentence so also is $p \vee q$, and from a non-ethical sentence p we can deduce $p \vee q$. There are also interesting cases that involve the logic of quantifiers.[4] Suppose we have the premiss that all teachers are members of a profession, then it follows that all teachers ought to do what all members of a profession ought to do.

There is obviously something fishy about such arguments from 'ought' to 'is'. They do not help us find direct guidance for action. A person who believes $p \vee q$ simply because he has deduced it from p has no reason to accept q or any other *useful* ethical sentence. Similarly a person who accepts that all teachers ought to do whatever all professionals ought to do still needs an ethical premiss (for example, 'No professional ought to go on strike') before he can deduce what teachers ought to do (for example, not go on strike).[5]

How should we rule out these fishy cases? Frank Jackson[6] has proposed two criteria of (respectively) 'factual invariance' and 'ethical invariance'. A valid argument is said by him to be 'factual invariant' if it remains valid when non-ethical terms are changed throughout for other non-ethical terms, and it is 'ethical invariant' if it remains valid when ethical terms are changed. Thus 'It is raining, therefore either it is raining or promises ought to be kept' remains valid even if 'raining' is changed throughout to (say) 'not raining'. Similarly, 'All teachers are professionals, therefore all teachers ought to do whatever all professionals ought to do' remains valid if 'ought' is replaced throughout by (say) 'ought not' or 'are permitted'. Factually invariant and ethically invariant deductions can then be ruled out as unwanted exceptions from the class of deductions envisaged by those who say that the ethical cannot be deduced from the factual.

Jackson gets into more difficult waters when he considers arguments of a rather different type, such as 'Joe did not kill Peter, therefore Joe did not murder Peter'. One has a feeling that the conclusion here follows from the premiss even though as it stands the argument is not validated by the rules of formal logic. We also have a feeling that the premiss is factual and the conclusion ethical. However if we can define 'murder' as 'wrongful killing' and if (following Donald Davidson[7]) we make a few syntactical transformations, we can get the following argument:

'There was not a killing of Peter by Joe, therefore there was not anything that was a killing of Peter by Joe and also wrongful'

which is of the form

$$\sim(\exists x)Fx \therefore \sim(\exists x)(Fx.Gx)$$

and of course valid. Nevertheless it can be ruled out by Jackson's criterion of factual invariance.

As I have indicated in my remarks about analyticity in Chapter I there is a question as to whether we can define 'murder' as 'wrongful killing'. To give such a definition is to suppose that murder has an *essence*, or that 'being wrongful' is *part of the meaning* of 'murder', or that 'murder is wrong' is *analytic*. If we reject notions of analyticity or of essence then there is no problem about Jackson's example, because we are then operating with a notion of logical consequence whereby 'Joe did not murder Peter' does not follow from 'Joe did not kill Peter', and so it does not matter whether 'murder' is or is not part of our ethical vocabulary. In either case we do not have a case of an ethical conclusion following in the required way from a non-ethical premiss.

Even a defender of the notion of analyticity might well reject the view that murder is always wrongful killing. Of course the satisfaction conditions of the predicate 'is wrongful' are context-dependent: for example an act may satisfy the predicate in a context of legal discourse and not in a context of moral discourse, and *vice versa*. Let us assume a context of moral discourse, as is relevant to our present concern. Then a person could hold that a certain act of euthanasia was a case of murder but not wrongful. (In this context the satisfaction conditions of 'murder' would be those of 'murder' in legal contexts.)

Jackson's defence of the autonomy of ethics depends on an ability to separate out an 'ethical' from a 'factual' vocabulary. But can ethics be separated from merely factual discourse by means of vocabulary? It should be noted also that Jackson's method could be adapted to give accounts of the autonomy of

Interlude on the naturalistic fallacy

law (by separating out legal from non-legal vocabulary) and of the autonomy of chemistry (by separating out chemical from, say, physical vocabulary), and so on. Perhaps we have lost the point behind the naturalistic fallacy. After all a naturalist might separate out an 'ethical' vocabulary from the rest of his 'factual' vocabulary, and produce a Jacksonian defence of the autonomy of ethics, not withstanding his naturalism.

When people say that 'ought' cannot be deduced from 'is' they are therefore thinking of something more than the logical and quasi-logical points that I have been discussing. Moore was thinking of ethical sentences as intimately connected with desire and action in a way in which factual sentences are connected rather with belief.

I want to rule out Moore's non-naturalism as scientifically and metaphysically unbelievable. But there are other theories of ethics, naturalism, emotivism, and imperativism, which do not seem to be quite right, but which seem to have something right about them. Thus it seems plausible that in a tribal or otherwise closed society the word 'ought' or its equivalent gets introduced to young children in a way that is quite 'factual'. (This is probably partly true of our own society.) They may learn '*A* is right' as having the truth conditions of 'This is commanded by the gods [the tribal elders, the Bible or whatever]'. Many philosophers will say that though children or people may learn to use words like 'ought' in a factual or legalistic sense, this is not the moral sense, because in the moral sense it is an open question whether what ought to be done possesses a certain naturalistic property. This brings us back to where we came in. Those who have wielded 'the naturalistic fallacy' as a dialectical weapon have elucidated it in such terms as 'open question', 'part of the meaning of', 'not inconsistent to say', 'it is not analytic that'. Yet if we reject such notions what is left of the debate about the naturalistic fallacy and about whether 'ought' can be deduced from 'is'?

RADICAL TRANSLATION AND ETHICS: SOME HEURISTIC CONSIDERATIONS

Quine has argued that there is no fact of the matter as to whether a given translation of another etymologically unrelated language

Interlude on the naturalistic fallacy

is correct (his thesis of the indeterminacy of translation). Similarly Donald Davidson has argued that the common-sense carving up of our dispositions into beliefs and desires respectively is indeterminate.[8] (The two theses of indeterminacy are not unconnected with one another.) I do not need to go so far as to accept either of these theses of indeterminacy. Quine's criticisms of the notion of analyticity, meaning, essence, necessity and so on are enough for my purpose. These do play havoc with the usual discussions of the naturalistic fallacy, 'ought' and 'is'. (Quine's and Davidson's additional theses of indeterminacy would of course add to this havoc in interesting ways.) Without committing myself on indeterminacy, I do wish to apply another Quinean notion, that of radical translation, to meta-ethics. I shall do so in a way that may bring out what is right and what is wrong in various meta-ethical theories, especially naturalism (both objectivist and subjectivist forms of it), emotivism and imperativism. On the question of the naturalistic fallacy, I want to suggest that it is not a clear question whether or not the naturalistic fallacy is a fallacy. Nevertheless, I would certainly want to argue that there is something suspect about any attempt to deduce ethical conclusions merely from propositions of natural science. It is possible for two people to agree on all matters of scientific fact, and yet to disagree about what ought to be done.

Consider an anthropologist who comes across an exotic people whose language is etymologically unrelated to any previously known language. How will the anthropologist set about translating, or at any rate paraphrasing, the natives' utterances? The anthropologist's problem is that of 'radical translation'.[9] A clear case of radical translation would have presented itself to Captain Cook, and later to the First Fleet, when the British first came to Australia and were confronted with the problem of interpreting various aboriginal languages. In the contemporary world I suppose that no clear cases of radical translation occur, though perhaps some anthropologists have to approximate to it. If ever we come in contact with extra-terrestrial intelligences, then either they will have to engage in radical translation of one of our languages, or else we will have to do the same for one of theirs. Radical translation has to be done without any dictionaries of the exotic language, and even without the etymological clues that might partly compensate for the lack of such dictionaries.

Interlude on the naturalistic fallacy

Our anthropologist will need to go about things in a comprehensive manner. Putting the matter loosely, we can say that the anthropologist will need hypotheses about beliefs, desires and meanings, and none of these sorts of hypotheses are independent of the others, and no particular hypothesis of any one of these sorts is independent of other hypotheses of that same sort. Thus, if an approach like that of Davidson is right, a theory of meaning is a theory of truth conditions for the language as a whole: meanings are not things that can be assigned to separate words or even sentences. Because in the situation of radical translation hypotheses must encompass beliefs, desires and meanings, linguistics and anthropology get mixed up with one another. The anthropologist cannot proceed piecemeal because the interpretation of one sentence will affect the interpretation of other sentences. Furthermore ascriptions of exotic beliefs will depend in part on interpretations of what the exotic people say, and behaviour is evidence for beliefs only relative to hypotheses about desires, and *vice versa*.

How will the anthropologist proceed? It is plausible that he or she can single out, with a fair degree of success, the observation sentences of the exotic language. He or she should apply various principles of charity: in particular he or she should apply the principle that the obvious should be translated by the obvious, modifying the application of this principle on occasion on account of the reflection that what may be obvious to the exotic interlocutor may not be obvious to the anthropologist, and *vice versa*.[10]

The anthropologist can also assume that the exotic people have basic desires, such as for food and water, similar to those that we have. He or she will also suppose that they, like us, believe obvious truths, such as that grass is green, that sugar is sweet, and that two and two are four. As I have said, the anthropologist must also remember that what is obvious to him or her need not be obvious to the exotic interlocutor, and indeed that something else may seem obvious to the exotic person. Various other constraints might be considered also as part of a strategy for narrowing down the infinite possibilities of translation presented by the unknown language. The anthropologist may also require, as Davidson does, that it should be possible to construct a recursive truth theory for the language that satisfies Tarski's

Interlude on the naturalistic fallacy

Convention T (⌜p⌝ is true if and only if p⌝). Or at any rate some recursive truth theory or other. Only with the aid of some such recursive theory can a necessarily finite translation manual allow us to deal with the potentially infinite set of sentences of a language.

Skipping familiar but difficult considerations of this sort, then, let us suppose that the anthropologist has gone some way towards preparing a translation manual for the exotic language. Suppose further the anthropologist has not as yet attempted to translate any sentences that according to some plausible classification would turn out to be ethical ones. Because the whole enterprise is holistic, subsequent success or failure to translate ethical sentences will of course react back on what he or she has done hitherto, so that he or she may have to modify the previously constructed part of the translation manual.

Let us suppose that anthropological investigations have suggested that the exotic people belong to a closed society of an authoritarian or theocratic nature, perhaps a tribal one. Our anthropologist may then be inclined by our anthropological knowledge of the society in question to hypothesize that some sentence S of the exotic language should be translated by some such sentence as 'We ought to tell the truth', if for example we ascertain that those who assent to this sentence also assent to 'Telling the truth is enjoined by the tribal elders', or perhaps 'Not telling the truth is punished by the gods'. Suppose secondly that the anthropologist's investigations suggest that the society is an atheistic, democratic and open one. Then we might adopt the policy of translating S as 'We ought to tell the truth' if and only if the people in question also assent to some sentence that we translate as 'Truth telling conduces to the total happiness', or something of that sort.

The success of such policies would not show that the exotic people use the word that the anthropologist translates as 'ought' in such a way that this word could be defined in terms of being enjoined by the tribal elders, of being punished by the gods, or of conducing to the general happiness. That is, the anthropologist would not espouse 'naturalistic' definitions of 'ought' and would recognise that even in such a society it is possible to deny such sentences as 'You ought to do what the tribal elders enjoin' or 'You ought not to do what the gods punish', or 'You ought to do

Interlude on the naturalistic fallacy

what leads to the maximum general happiness'. That is, it is not linguistically inappropriate to dissent from any of these statements. This is the truth that lies behind Moore's use of the 'open question' argument.

Would the success of such a policy show that the exotic people were using their word for 'ought' in such a way that it could be defined in terms of being enjoined by the tribal elders, not being punished by the gods, or conducing to the maximum general happiness, or whatever as the case may be? Surely not. We must suppose that the equivalent in the exotic language of 'You ought to do what the tribal elders enjoin', or 'You ought not to do what the gods punish', or whatever, is not a tautology, and that it is not linguistically inappropriate for them to ask whether they ought to do what the tribal elders enjoin, or whatever. Compare the case of scientific terms. As was noted in Chapter 1, it might have been plausible at one time to say that 'atom' was just shorthand for 'indivisible particle of matter'. This would nevertheless have been wrong or misleading: as science developed there was no difficulty about talk of atoms being made up of smaller particles, of splitting the atom, and so on. It was therefore to some extent always an open question whether atoms were indivisible: the most one can say is that there used to be a time when the assertion that atoms are indivisible was very well entrenched in what Quine has called 'the web of belief'.

These considerations about radical translation may enable us to see what is right and what is wrong with both the naturalist (definist) position and the non-naturalist position. Another consideration is as follows. In radical translation of moral discourse we would normally be (more or less) reluctant to translate an exotic sentence as 'I ought to do so-and-so' if the speaker did not appear to have any desire to do so-and-so. (Such a desire might of course be outweighed by other desires, selfish ones for example.) This shows what both emotivist theories of ethics, that ethical sentences are an *expression* of feelings or attitudes;[11] and subjectivist theories, that ethical sentences *report* our feelings or attitudes, are confusedly getting at. Similarly, a person who uttered a sentence translated by the anthropologist as 'You ought to do so-and-so' would be likely to be happy also to utter a sentence that should be translated as 'Do so-and-so'. This shows the partial truth in the prescriptivist or imperativist theory,

Interlude on the naturalistic fallacy

that ethical sentences express commands, requests, and the like. Emotivism, and to a lesser extent subjectivism, have trouble over ethical sentences that occur in subordinate clauses, and imperativist theories have trouble over sentences like 'Caesar did some things he ought not to have done'. (I shall return to this matter later.)

In practice, interpretation of an exotic language is rarely, if ever, radical, since nowadays the complete etymological isolation that it presupposes is rarely if ever found. (It would be found if we were to get into communication with an extra-terrestrial species.) If it could occur, or to the extent that an approximation to it can in fact occur, the success or failure of the various tactics for translating ethical language would testify to the partial correctness of the various theories of ethics to which these tactics correspond. As it is, I use the idea as an expository device, to indicate how a theory of ethical language could avoid the usual talk in terms of 'meaning', 'synonymy', 'property', 'analyticity', and the like.

Such a theory of ethics would be to some extent reconciliationist, and might be compared with a reconciliationist move that A.N. Prior, following Ernest and Maria Clark, explores on page 11 of his *Logic and the Basis of Ethics*.[12] The idea is that sometimes when we call a thing 'good' we may mean that it is pleasant, at other times that it promotes survival, at other times that it is what we desire, and so on for a number of other characteristics. When an ethical naturalist gives some one of these characteristics as the connotation of 'good' we feel dissatisfied because the other meanings are at the back of our mind. Thus, if it is said that promoting survival is good we may take this as significant, namely as meaning that promoting survival is what we desire, and if we say that what we desire is good we may take this as significant, namely as meaning that what we desire promotes survival. And so on. It seems to me that the reconciliationist approach through the notion of radical translation has the advantage over that of the Clarks in not implying a subjectivist theory of meaning and in not requiring us to talk of attributes, characteristics, meanings, or other entities of that sort. Moreover, it does some justice to what is good in emotivism and prescriptivism.

Interlude on the naturalistic fallacy

A RECENT FORM OF INTUITIONISM

Earlier in the chapter I objected to Moore's non-naturalism partly on the grounds that it implied an epistemology of synthetic *a priori* intuition that is incompatible with a mechanistic and biological view of human kind. A more subtle form of intuitionism has been recently put forward by various writers.[13] I propose to extract a theory from my reading of these authors. I find them hard to understand, and so I do not claim to have got the theory quite right or in a form which they would totally support. But as far as I can understand the theory it is this. Goodness is supervenient on perfectly natural properties, but it is not itself non-natural, and does not require any non-natural epistemological apparatus for us to perceive its occurrence.

That is, if something good has a certain set of natural properties (or if a certain set of natural predicates are true of it) then any other object which had this set of properties would be good too. Nevertheless there are no laws relating goodness and natural properties. There are no laws of nature relating (essentially) to goodness much as there are no laws of nature relating (essentially) to tables. What is a table is a matter of our interests in sitting at meals, writing letters, surveying (plane tables), and so on. There is also some 'open texture'.[14] Is a carpenter's bench a table? There are perhaps more or less accidental generalizations, but such generalizations are not laws. Consider 'All tables have flat tops'. I do not know whether this is true, but we can imagine (within the bounds of physical possibility) badly made tables with pyramidal tops, or table tops with all sorts of ups and downs for the purpose of some game, for example. Of course there are laws, or at least law-like generalizations that are inessentially about tables. For example, if two tables collide in mid-air then momentum will be conserved. But this is a mere specification of the law 'If two objects collide then momentum will be conserved'. There are no laws that would justify us in treating tables as a 'natural kind' (to use a phrase that for reasons I need not go into here I do not altogether like). And yet if one object is exactly like another in its physical constitution and structure, then if one is a table then the other is also a table. Tableness is 'supervenient'.

Interlude on the naturalistic fallacy

The writers in question hold that goodness is able to be *perceived*, just as the property of being a table is, but their form of intuitionism does not rely on any 'supernatural' sort of intuition. There are properties that have an importance for us as human beings: the ability to detect them may have been built into us by evolution, or it may have come about by early training. We often misperceive a twig as a snake: snakiness has an obvious biological importance for us. We do not perceive mere sense data as 'snakey' sense data: indeed philosophers are now mostly agreed that we do not perceive sense data at all. We perceive physical objects, and our perception brings information that goes beyond that carried by sensory stimulation. It is as if observation was always tinged with hypothesis. So similarly, according to this theory, we can directly perceive the supervenient property of goodness, though the information flow (photons entering the eyes, etc.) is no more than that brought about by the *sub*venient or merely physical properties. So according to this theory, goodness is supervenient but can be detected with our ordinary senses, our eyes and ears.

The difficulty here is to see what this theory comes to. It is useful to compare it with the theory of Ernest and Maria Clark, which I mentioned earlier in this chapter. In view of the frequent disagreements between people of different ethical views, in the way in which they ascribe goodness or refuse to ascribe it, the supervenience theory does not seem to me to do justice to the partial insights of emotivism and subjectivism. (The Clark view can at least partially accommodate subjectivism.) It is true that the supervenience theory does stress the way in which perception is conditioned by our interests: it is presumably because of our interest in not being bitten that we perceive snakes more readily than we perceive birds – or at any rate they present us with a much more vivid feeling of a 'snakey' quality than (normally) birds are presented to us as 'birdy'. So the idea is that our interests have led us, either as a result of evolution or of training, to single out a certain complex of properties (for which there are no necessary and sufficient conditions, but which we add to or subtract from according to a certain psychological naturalness). Wiggins has compared the process to that discussed by Wittgenstein on 'following a rule'.[15] In the case of the theory of Ernest and Maria Clark the more natural suggestion is to relate it to

Interlude on the naturalistic fallacy

Wittgenstein's notion of family resemblance concepts. The idea would be that 'good' corresponds to a cluster of properties, none of which are necessary or sufficient for goodness.[16] Thus it might be held that provided a thing has a number of certain properties in the cluster (say, being conducive to pleasure, being approved of by most people, being approved by the speaker) a person will correctly apply the term 'good'. A similar but more complicated story might be given for 'ought'. (For sources of complication see Chapter 4.) If so, as Wiggins says, we 'desire x because we think x good' and yet it is equally the case that 'x is good because we desire x'.[17] The trouble is that we could single out an objective goodness in this way only if there were a similarity of human interests like the similarity of (most) human beings in their reactions to snakes. A greater concession to subjectivism or non-cognitivism would seem to be needed to account for the differences in ultimate moral judgments which do seem as a matter of fact to exist. Compare someone who does and someone who does not stress justice at the expense of total utility. Such differences (aided perhaps by differences in philosophical confusion) account for the fact that there are many systems of morality, the differences of one from another being often only partially accountable to differences in empirical beliefs or the situations in which the moral systems in question are put into practice.

The supervenience theory is not only about goodness. It is also about our perception of such qualities as kindness, loyalty and courage. Surely one must agree that these are in a sense supervenient: they are not behaviouristically definable in any tight way. No doubt they are states of the brain, but not identifiable with any tightly defined set of neurological properties. (Even though any particular instantiation of such a property is identical to a certain neurological state. The theory is compatible with a physicalist metaphysics.) No doubt one is able immediately to see behaviour as kind or loyal or courageous. We can also say that kindness, loyalty and courage are ethical properties, since they are of particular interest to moralists. Nevertheless G.E. Moore would consider them as natural – not non-natural or ethical. No doubt there have been fierce tribes who have thought kindness evil, and pacific ones that have not been too keen on courage. So the modern 'intuitionism' that I am

Interlude on the naturalistic fallacy

discussing bears very little similarity to Moore's. My main worry about it is that it does not do justice, as emotivism does, to disagreement about ultimate ethical principle or even to differences in ethical 'perception'. Or if it is modified so as to do so, then it is not as objectivist as one would expect an 'intuitionist' theory to be.

SOME REMARKS ON EMOTIVISM AND IMPERATIVISM

I have alluded in the previous section to what is good and bad about emotivism and imperativism. However, I feel that it is incumbent on me to say a little bit more about these theories.[18]

The emotive theory arose through a modification of subjectivism, the theory that 'This is good' means the same as 'I approve of this'. Subjectivism naturally had fallen foul of the objection that the theory implies that if one person says 'This is good' and another says 'This is not good' (or 'This is bad'), they would not be contradicting one another. Yet they certainly seem to be contradicting one another: there is a disagreement between them. The answer of the emotivists, of whom C.L. Stevenson had the most thoroughly worked-out theory of this sort, was that when someone says that something is good he or she is not primarily *reporting* that he or she has an attitude of approval to that thing: he or she is *expressing* such an attitude. There is a disagreement between someone who says that something is good and someone who says that this same thing is bad, but the disagreement is not a disagreement in belief. The disagreement is not about the truth or falsity of a proposition, but is a disagreement in attitude. The disagreement is analogous to that which might be expressed at the end of a political election, when supporters of one side might cry 'Hurrah' and supporters of the other side might cry 'Boo'.

The emotive theory quickly was extended to something that might be confused with the imperativist theory. Thus Ayer, after saying in his *Language, Truth and Logic* that to say 'Stealing money is wrong' is much like saying 'Stealing money!!' in a particular tone of horror, goes on to say that ethical utterances are calculated not only to express our feelings but to arouse feelings in others, and compares 'You ought to tell the truth' with 'Tell the truth'.[19] Similarly C.L. Stevenson suggests that a first

Interlude on the naturalistic fallacy

approximation to the analysis of some uses of 'This is good' is as follows: 'I approve of this: do so as well'.[20] For the moment I shall neglect this reference to imperatives until I remark on the imperativist theory itself.

The first thing to notice about the emotive theory is that its name suggests that an ethical utterance is some sort of explosion, like the utterance of a swear word, so that what it expresses is an emotion in the sense of 'agitation'[21] or 'excited mental state'.[22] However, Ayer's move towards the imperative theory and Stevenson's move to saying that ethical statements typically express 'attitudes' go some way towards recognizing that ethical sentences have nothing in particular to do with the expression of emotions. Certainly they may express emotions, as in Ayer's example 'Stealing money!!' but they need not: one is not expressing any excited mental state, one of what Hume called 'the violent passions', when one says that on balance one ought to give a sum of money to a certain charity. Indeed one may feel very strongly that one ought to give the money to a certain charity without getting excited or emotional. To use an analogy of Ryle's, the flow of a stream can be very strong and yet can have no eddies, and it can be relatively weak and yet full of turbulence. Emotions and attitudes are things of different kinds.[23] The psychology of the emotive theory has been of course bedevilled by the fact that expression of feeling may be taken to be expression of emotion, but also more plausibly for the theory, merely as expression of attitude (as often in Jane Austen, for example). To use an example given to me by J.O. Urmson, suppose that one (a) reads in the paper that there has been a massacre in Nicaragua and (b) more or less simultaneously notices that someone has been spitting on the carpet. A feeling of outrage may arise about (b) and yet one will surely feel that (a) constitutes an evil of incomparably greater magnitude, even though no strong feeling arises in us – unfortunately we have got anaesthetized to reading of horrors in the newspapers. This anaesthetization is connected with the fact that we cannot do anything to prevent these remote horrors: if we could we would get much more agitated until we were able to put our desires into action. But if we *could* do something about the massacre and had a choice as to whether to do something about it or to do something about the mess on the carpet we would of course

Interlude on the naturalistic fallacy

enthusiastically see to the matter of the massacre and completely forget about the carpet or the mess on it. In this way an attitude theory is stronger than a literally 'emotive' theory.

Indeed it is sentences that have meaning, or can be the subject matter of a truth theory.[24] It is of course the case that the phenomenon of indexicality forces us to relativize truth to a person and a time, so that, for example, the sentence 'I will play cricket' said by P at t is true if and only if P plays cricket later than t. We can have a non-relative characterization of the truth of a particular *utterance*, since any utterance must be by a particular person at a time. Nevertheless in semantics it is better to talk of sentences rather than of utterances, if only for the reason that there are infinitely many well-formed sentences that never have been or will be uttered. Moreover, even if we do count utterances as objects of a semantic theory, it is not in their semantic capacity as such that utterances may express emotion. 'I ought to give money' can be uttered on some occasions emotively and on others dispassionately, and 'He's arrived' can sometimes be uttered dispassionately and sometimes emotively. A particular utterance may be emotive only in the way that any action can be emotive – one utterance can be emotive and another not, one avoidance of a snake can be calm and another excited. Whether ethical sentences more often express emotions than do sentences of (say) natural history is a matter for sociologists of language more than for theorists of meaning.

What is it to 'express' an emotion? We must not think of an emotion as a mysterious gas or vapour at high pressure, and the expression of it as a sort of hissing out of this gas or vapour through a suddenly released valve. To say that the utterance of a sentence S expresses an emotion is to say that we can guess from a description of the utterance that the person had that emotion. Thus the assertion that someone said 'There's a snake' in a highly distraught tone of voice implies (with high probability) that the utterer of the sentence was frightened of the snake. 'There's a snake' does not imply this itself. Similarly with expression of attitude and of belief. We may deduce that someone is fond of symbolic logic from the fact of his or her assertion that symbolic logic is good stuff, but not from 'Symbolic logic is good stuff' itself. We can also deduce the same thing from facts that do not have anything to do with utterance, such as that the person in

Interlude on the naturalistic fallacy

question spends a lot of his leisure time working out problems in symbolic logic. Again we deduce that someone believes that it is going to rain not from his assertion 'It is going to rain' itself, but from the fact that the person makes that assertion.

Such a deduction is no more than probabilistic, even though it can give conviction near to certainty. Apart from the fact that a person may be lying about his belief that it will rain (doubtless in this example for some rather unusual reason!) he may suffer from self-deception, and give an incorrect account of his state of mind. Nevertheless from the fact that a person sincerely assents to a sentence it is reasonable to say that he believes it to be true (or if the sentence is indexical, true relative to a person and a time). So in the context of radical translation the fact that a person is likely to believe what he says does provide a canon of use in *interpreting* his assertions. We say that his utterances 'express his beliefs'. Similarly they can express his attitudes too, in the sense that the fact that he utters a sentence may give us ground for probabilistically ascribing an attitude to him. These considerations show how a reasonable view of what it is to express an attitude differs from notions like 'giving vent to an emotion', 'letting off steam'. Roughly speaking the notion of 'expressing' is epistemic, while that of 'giving vent to' is psychological.

Radical translation involves simultaneous solving for beliefs, attitudes or desires, and meanings (in the sense appropriate to 'truth theories').[25] This explains how the attitudes expressed by complex sentences can be functions of the attitudes expressed by their components. To take a simple case, it explains why 'This is not good' expresses an attitude opposite to that of 'This is good', and, if our semantics can cope with counterfactual conditionals, how 'good' does not express a pro-attitude in the context: 'If Hitler had been good the war would not have occurred'. The emotive theory itself is in trouble, since it has to suppose that inserting a 'not' in a sentence is like turning off a tap, and goodness knows what hydraulic analogies might be appropriate in the cases of more complex sentences! Similarly the emotive theory has difficulty in dealing with quantification into ethical contexts. Suppose that I say 'Some of Julius Caesar's actions were right'. Of which actions of his am I expressing approval? I may have been told that some of Julius Caesar's actions were right, but I might not know which these were. The emotive

Interlude on the naturalistic fallacy

theory would need unnatural and very strained paraphrases even to begin to deal with such an example. On the view of expression as a sort of letting off steam, these things would be mysterious, rather as if the utterance of 'not' should turn a valve in the brain! It is not without interest in this connection that Stevenson held to a causal theory of meaning rather than a semantic one, in the sense in which semantics is the theory of truth and denotation. I have noted, however, that because of his 'Do so as well' he might (rather confusedly) suggest an imperativist theory. Provided that we have a semantics for imperatives, perhaps parasitic on one for indicatives, as was suggested in Chapter 1, puzzles about 'expression' disappear. We do not need to worry about what attitudes are 'expressed' by the utterance of imperatives but can go straight to the semantics of these imperatives themselves.

We can of course concede to the emotivists that there are words whose use in itself tends to arouse feelings, regardless of what is actually asserted in the sentences that contain them. 'Nigger' is a good example. Note, however, that the case in question here is very different from that of 'good' and 'right'. It would be felt as almost as insulting to the black community to say of someone that he was *not* a nigger as it would be to say that he *was* a nigger. The propensity of 'nigger' to arouse feeling may depend partly on convention, but nevertheless it gives rise to a direct causal effect that is independent of the semantics of sentences in which it occurs.

In the case of imperatives too, we must distinguish the question of the causal effects of utterances of them from the semantics of the imperatives themselves. The semantics of 'Shut the door' has to do with what sort of action on the part of the addressee complies with the utterance, and this can be stated without going into the causal question of whether the utterance of the imperative tends to cause the addressee to shut the door, or whatever.

Because of the availability of a semantics for imperatives the imperativist theory can deal easily with some of the difficulties which beset the emotive theory. The semantic relation of 'You ought . . .' and 'You ought not . . .' can be elucidated by means of the relation between 'Do . . .' and 'Do not . . .'. 'If you ought to do X, you ought to do Y' can be elucidated if we allow our syntax for imperatives to be extended to cover sentences of the

Interlude on the naturalistic fallacy

form 'If do X, then do Y'. But imperativist theories cannot do very well with sentences involving quantification into 'ought' or 'good' contexts, for example 'Some of Caesar's actions were good' or 'The admiral sometimes did what he ought'. It will not do to render this as 'Approve of some of Caesar's actions' or 'Approve of some of the admiral's deeds'. One could comply with these imperatives by approving of some of Caesar's or the admiral's wrong deeds. Moreover one can assent to these sentences without knowing *which* of Caesar's or the admiral's actions were good or right.

The matter of quantification into 'ought' contexts relates also to the matter of the universality of imperatives. The compliance conditions of an imperative relate contextually to the class of addresses of the imperative. Thus, as Hare has remarked,[26] 'Honour thy father and mother' was supposed to be addressed to the chosen people. However, there is no reason in principle why imperatives should not be addressed to all human beings, or even to all rational beings in the universe, terrestrial or extra-terrestrial, whether bipeds or (possibly?) dolphins and whales (certain practical difficulties excepted, of course).

Both the emotive and imperative theories run up against the sort of difficulty raised by Stevenson when he considers the sentence

> 'It is (morally) right for him to be exceptionally charitable, but not his duty or obligation – nothing that he positively ought to do.'[27]

Here if 'right' and 'not his duty or obligation' express attitudes they would seem to express contrary ones at the same time, and if they stand in for imperatives they would seem to stand in for inconsistent ones. (Stevenson's own answer to the problem here is rather weak.) Of course whether such a sentence would be uttered depends on a person's normative ethics. A utilitarian would not recognize the distinction between dutiful actions and supererogatory ones. What one should do, according to the utilitarian, is to maximize the general happiness or whatever, and this leaves no room for supererogation. What the utilitarian would say would be something like 'One ought not to blame people for not being exceptionally charitable, even though they ought to be exceptionally charitable'. There would, on the

Interlude on the naturalistic fallacy

emotive theory, be no conflict of expressed attitude here. Nevertheless, a meta-ethical theory ought to cover a variety of normative ethical discourse, both utilitarian and non-utilitarian.

Despite the defects of imperativism, and still more of emotivism, I am anxious to preserve something of what they are getting at. Emotivism was bedevilled in the hands of Stevenson by confusing semantics and pragmatics. Nevertheless the pragmatics of ethical language is not unimportant. Indeed in the next chapter I shall be concerned with the pragmatics of ethical persuasion, which raises a certain puzzle about why distinctively ethical language is needed at all.

III

WHY MORAL LANGUAGE?

MORAL LANGUAGE AS INFLUENCING ACTION

This chapter will be concerned with the rather central employment of ethical language in which the user of ethical words is trying to influence the conduct of his audience, either by putting forward universal judgments, such as 'Everyone ought to honour his or her father and mother', or by the corresponding imperative, such as 'Honour your father and mother'. Persuasion may also be achieved less directly by evaluating traits of persons or of character, as in 'Jones is an evil man', which may have the force of 'Don't have anything to do with Jones, because he is an evil man'. In such cases we are using ethical language in order to *persuade*. Persuasion is a matter for the pragmatics of ethical language, rather than its semantics, and in this chapter I want to concentrate on pragmatic issues. One question that will arise is of how much we need ethical words such as 'ought'. In the previous chapter I have thrown some doubt on whether there is a fact of the matter as to whether the naturalistic fallacy is a fallacy; but to the extent that 'ought' statements are not uniquely determined by 'is' statements (as in an open society) we can still speak, as M. Zimmerman has done, of the 'is-ought' barrier. (I shall of course ignore those pathological cases of deduction of 'ought' from 'is' that were discussed in the last chapter, for example, the deduction of '$p \vee q$' from 'p', where 'p' is an 'is' statement and 'q' an 'ought' statement.) I have in mind here one of the most stimulating papers that have been written on moral philosophy

Why moral language?

for more than twenty years, in which Zimmerman argues for the uselessness of moral language.[1]

ZIMMERMAN'S REJECTION OF MORAL LANGUAGE

Does the supposed 'is-ought' barrier matter? Zimmerman says 'No' because he holds that we could get on perfectly well in our moral life without 'ought' statements or similar moral terminology. Zimmerman is thinking of the persuasive function of moral language, and is thinking of fairly direct statements, such as 'You ought to do X' in which the indicative sentence functions much like the imperative sentence 'Do X' in so far as for the speaker a satisfactory conclusion to the transaction between speaker and hearer would normally be the hearer's actually doing X. Things are not so simple in the case of other sorts of 'ought' statements, such as 'Napoleon ought not to have invaded Russia', in which the connection between assent and action is much less clear.

Suppose I say to you, out of the blue, 'You ought to do X'. Why should you do X just because I say that you ought to do it? Similarly, if I utter the imperative sentence 'Do X' when I have no legal or customary (quasi-legal) authority over you, why should this weigh with you? The case is different, of course, if 'Do X' is said by a sergeant, say, to a corporal or a private soldier. The mere fact that an order is given by a military superior gives the addressee a motive to comply with it. At the very least the addressee will have a prudential motive to comply with the order. Or again, the addressee might have a disinterested desire to comply with the conventions of military life, in which the giving and receiving of orders plays such an important part. The addressee may have a disinterested desire for the smooth running of the military system.

Zimmerman considers the case of a judge who is called upon to sentence a prisoner who has been found guilty of killing his wife and children in order to collect their life insurance. We might be inclined to say that the judge ought to sentence the prisoner. Suppose, however, that we refuse to accept 'ought' statements. We may think that 'ought' statements cannot be derived from 'is' statements, and that only 'is' statements can be objectively

Why moral language?

justified, for example by scientific evidence. So we do not have the option of saying that the judge ought to sentence the prisoner. Does this matter? Zimmerman's answer is 'No'. We know that the judge wants to sentence the prisoner and that we want the judge to sentence the prisoner. Why does the judge want to sentence the prisoner? One reason might be that the judge wants to deter other potential murderers, and sentencing the prisoner will help to deter such potential murderers. At the very least, as Zimmerman points out, the judge wants to remain a judge, and the judge is unlikely to remain a judge if he or she refuses to sentence the prisoner. (I shall ignore the question of whether Zimmerman may have underestimated the security of tenure of judges!) In saying all this we are entirely within the realm of 'is' statements. 'Is' statements can affect the beliefs of those who accept them, and if they are questioned they can be supported by other and more acceptable 'is' statements. If a person does not want to do X, and cannot be brought to want to do X by the adducing of 'is' statements, for example the statement that doing X is a means to Y which the person already wants, then he or she will not be persuaded to do X. It would seem that the mere uttering of 'ought' sentences or imperative sentences, such as 'You ought to sentence the prisoner' or 'Sentence the prisoner', is not going to help. Why should Smith do X just because Jones says to him 'You ought to do X'? In persuading someone to do X we must appeal to his desires, and we can do so directly by means of 'is' statements that state or imply that a certain course of action will conduce to the satisfaction of these desires. To say 'You ought to do X' will not influence action unless (a) the addressee thinks that what is said is true and (b) he or she has a generalized desire to do what he or she ought as such. If 'ought' does not follow from 'is' there is a puzzle as to why (a) should hold, and even if (a) held there would be a puzzle as to why we should believe (b) to hold. If 'ought' were not a matter of desires a person might agree in an intellectual way that he or she ought to do X, and yet might have no desire to bring about X. A man might dislike the obligatory just as another might dislike sugar in his tea.

If then our purpose in moral discourse is to persuade people to act in certain ways, it would appear that 'ought' statements are unnecessary and that we can keep to the point better without them. To revert to the example of the judge, surely, as Zimmerman suggests, it would be more efficacious to say to a wavering judge 'If you do not sentence the prisoner you will not deter potential murderers' or 'If you do not sentence the prisoner you will not long remain a judge' than it would be to say 'You ought to sentence the prisoner'. Similarly an economic adviser to an Australian minister might say 'If you cut tariffs you will raise unemployment in the clothing industry'. Assuming that the minister has a desire to avoid unemployment in the clothing industry nothing would be gained by the adviser saying in addition 'You *ought* not to cut tariffs'. And if the minister, surprisingly, does not mind raising unemployment in the clothing industry, he or she is not going to take any notice of the adviser's 'You ought not . . .' either. Of course another adviser might bring in another consideration, such as that to keep tariffs will harm clothing workers in south-east Asian countries, which will not be able to sell their manufactured clothing so cheaply in Australia as they would if there were no tariffs. But once again, if the minister does not want to increase the prosperity of workers in south-east Asian countries nothing will be gained by the adviser saying 'You ought to cut tariffs'. Why should the minister cut tariffs just because the adviser says that the minister ought to? And if the minister *does* want to help the workers in south-east Asian countries then the factual assertions of the adviser should be enough to guide action, if the minister is convinced that they can be reasonably supported in the usual ways that factual assertions can be supported.

In seeking to persuade someone to a course of action of which we approve, then, we try to canalize this person's desires in the appropriate direction by making factual remarks relevant to the direction of his desires. To go on to say 'You ought to . . .' seems to be an additional and empty piece of rhetoric. Alternatively, if a statement of the form 'You ought to . . .' had any function over and above that of the statement of the relevant facts that might canalize the addressee's desires, we should be confronted with the 'is-ought' barrier to which Zimmerman refers.

It might now be contended, in opposition to Zimmerman, that surely we can have a desire to do what we ought, simply because we ought, and that this ethically ultimate desire is what can be canalized by 'ethical information' to the effect that such and such

Why moral language?

is what we ought to do. Cannot such an ethical desire be canalized by an assertion of ethical fact just as a desire to avoid causing unemployment or to help the prosperity of workers in south-east Asia may be canalized by an assertion of economic fact?

Philosophers who adopt this position often suppose that ethical information can canalize an ethical desire just as ordinary factual information can canalize ordinary desires. The ethical desire to do what we ought can be canalized by the information that (for example) we ought to relieve unhappiness, just as the desire to go to a grocer's shop (say) may be canalized by the information that there is a grocer's shop in the High Street.

There are at least two odd things about this sort of story. One is that it raises the question of how we could get acquainted with these supposed ethical facts. Propositions asserting such ethical facts are sometimes supposed to be synthetic *a priori*, known by a faculty of ethical intuition. Such a faculty of intuition does not fit in with a biological or naturalistic view of man. If the mind is, roughly speaking, the brain, how could it get in contact in an *a priori* manner with non-natural properties and synthetic connections? How could a biologically oriented and neuro-physiological psychology explain such a mysterious thing? (Recall my discussion of Moore in Chapter 2.) Ordinary facts (for example, scientific ones) are known either by observation or by proposing hypotheses that explain observations. It is not clear how there could be ethical observations or an ethical hypothetico-deductive method based on such ethical observations. Attempts by philosophers to avoid the synthetic *a priori* by basing ethics on respect for persons, 'original positions', the meaning of the moral words, or of the word 'moral' itself, all smuggle substantive ethical assumptions into their premisses.

Another odd thing about the story about ethical facts is that if it were true then a person could sincerely say that he or she ought to do a certain action and yet have not the least tendency or desire to do the action. He or she could say that this sort of action had the property of obligatoriness, but that as a matter of fact he or she had a dislike for this property. In appealing to such a perception of the ethical fact we would have to appeal also to a presumably contingent extra fact, namely that we happen to have a tendency to do actions of a sort we perceive to have the property of obligatoriness. Why should we need such perception of ethical fact as the ultimate canalizers of our desires and why should we have such specifically ethical desires? As was noted earlier, our desires can be canalized by perfectly ordinary empirical beliefs.

The uselessness of 'ought' statements would also appear to be equally plausible if we accepted a non-cognitivist view of 'ought' statements, assimilating 'ought' statements to imperatives or to expressions of attitude. If our desires do get canalized as the result of an imperative or expression of attitude they are not canalized by a belief expressed by the imperative or by a mere expression of attitude, since no beliefs are expressed by it. They are canalized by the belief that the utterance of such a sentence engenders in us about the speaker's desires, of which we may want to take account. In this case, however, the same effect could be achieved without the use of an 'ought' sentence. The speaker could say 'You will make me most unhappy if you do so and so' or 'If you do such and such I shall be very pleased'. (I am of course here ignoring cases, such as those of commands in the army, in which the imperative mood – or perhaps the imperatival future as in 'The battalion will move at first light' – can confer a certain legal or quasi-legal status on the utterance.) Thus a professor may not persuade his or her vice-chancellor by the bulldozing language of 'You ought not to do so and so', but the professor may, if he or she is fortunate, get somewhere by saying that he or she will be most upset if a certain thing is done. Here the professor apprises the vice-chancellor of a certain fact that may modify the vice-chancellor's desires in a certain way. On the other hand it may not so modify them, because the vice-chancellor may not mind the professor in question getting upset, or if the vice-chancellor does mind it he or she may not mind it as much as he or she would mind changing his or her plan of action.

Thus we can see the strength of Zimmerman's view that we could get on perfectly well in contexts of moral argument and persuasion even if we avoided the use of specifically moral words. If he is right then he is also right in saying that there need be no 'is-ought' barrier to cross. Nevertheless we may still feel uneasy. If specifically moral language is as unnecessary as Zimmerman suggests it is, then there is surely a puzzle about the prevalence of words like 'ought' in actual languages. Why have moral words preserved their place in language as language has evolved over centuries? Indeed how did they get into moral language in the first place?

CONSIDERATIONS ABOUT THE LANGUAGE OF 'OUGHT'

The 'is-ought' gap is similar to the 'indicative-imperative' gap Zimmerman's argument that 'ought' statements are dispensable would equally show that imperatives are dispensable, except in legal or quasi-legal or otherwise authoritarian situations. Indeed 'ought' statements shade naturally into imperatives *via* 'shalt' statements. It does not much matter whether Jehovah said 'You ought not to worship any other god but me' or whether he said 'Do not worship any other god but me' or whether he said the intermediate sounding 'Thou shalt not . . .' as in the English Revised Version of the New Testament, which I gather here follows the grammar of Hebrew. Acquiescence in the commandments was natural because of belief in the power and awesomeness of Jehovah. It is natural to see morality as having issued out of religion, so that notions of the autonomy of morals are a late development. Autonomous morality rests ultimately on the desires of agents. These need not be selfish desires of course: they can be desires to obey a god or desires to promote the happiness of all sentient beings, for example. Originally religious (non-autonomous) ethics would have rested ultimately on the supposed desires of a god or gods, and acquiescence in furthering these supposed desires would have depended on emotions of fear or love of a numinous being.

This suggests that the puzzle about why we need 'ought' statements can at least in part be answered by the consideration that for certain purposes 'ought' statements carry with them a quasi-religious cloud of numinous feeling. In this way, as Elizabeth Anscombe has said, utterances of 'ought' statements come to be felt as *authoritative*, even after a religious context for them has been lost.[2] J.L. Mackie has preferred a rather different explanation: he has suggested that the ordinary meaning of terms such as 'ought' (in ethical contexts) is both objective and prescriptive: thus an ethical 'ought' sentence is felt both as stating a truth about the universe (a 'non-natural' truth in something like G.E. Moore's sense) and *also* as carrying prescriptive force like a command.[3] Mackie thus holds that ordinary ethical discourse is laden with a false metaphysical theory (the theory of non-natural qualities or relations). Moreover it is hard to see how any statement of fact could be prescriptive independently of our desires, and it is hard to see how a belief about non-natural facts would be any the more efficacious in guiding our desires than would a belief about natural facts. In either case we must want to bring about the truth of certain propositions, whether they be 'non-natural' ones or whether they be 'natural' ones.

Mackie interestingly suggests that the spurious objectivity of moral language comes about because of a certain confusion of mind whereby we 'project' our feelings on to the external world. Some philosophers have held that colours really belong to our sense data and that we project them on the world, so that the brilliant hues of a sunset do not belong to the external world but are generated by the mind of the perceiver. I believe that this is an incorrect view about colours, of which I would give a physicalist account,[4] but this does not matter for the present purpose. Mackie holds that just as according to this view colours are projected on to the outside world, non-natural ethical properties are not part of the objective world, though we have a tendency to think falsely that they are, because of the way we project our feelings or desires.

Of course this talk of 'projection' is somewhat metaphorical: feelings are not projectiles that the mind throws at an external reality, nor are they like the slide of a magic lantern. Mackie elucidates the idea of projection by means of that of reversing our views about dependence: instead of thinking of goodness as depending on our desires we think of our desires as depending on goodness. Mackie's analysis does importantly draw attention to the way in which 'ought' statements can be used so as to take advantage of intellectual confusion in the addressee. Even if I have no authority over you, my saying 'You ought to . . .' may seem more authoritative to you than would my saying something factual. If I say to you 'If you do A then B will result' (which is a factual statement) it will cut no ice with you if you are aware that you do not want B anyway, but the numinousness of 'ought' may cause in you some desire to do A if I say in an authoritative tone,

Why moral language?

and if I seem to be someone who knows what's what, 'You ought to do '*A*' '.

Nevertheless it is hard to believe that moral words retain their place in the language entirely because of such confusion of mind. In Chapter 6 I shall give a semantical explanation of something *like* Mackie's theory of projection, but without the metaphysical and numinous elements on which Mackie lays stress. Words like 'ought' and 'right' are used quite happily in non-moral contexts and without any feeling of the numinous or of the non-natural. Consider the sentence 'If you want to get that thing off you ought to use a Phillips head screwdriver'. Such sentences have traditionally been said to express 'hypothetical imperatives'. In a hypothetical imperative the 'If you want . . .' and 'you ought' may be thought of as cancelling one another out, so that we are left with a statement of fact. But if the 'If you want . . .' and 'you ought . . .' do cancel one another out, why do we have this language at all? Why not say 'Getting that thing off is most easily done by using a Phillips head screwdriver'? What need was there for 'ought' in the first place?

Well, suppose that it was not the case that the *easiest* way to get the thing off was by using a Phillips head screwdriver, but that any other method would damage the head of the screw. In that case we should need a different replacement for our hypothetical imperative. We should need the factual statement 'Getting that thing off without using a Phillips screwdriver will damage the head of the screw'. Thus, depending on the facts of the case, there is a variety of statements that might be used instead of the hypothetical imperative. Note that all the relevant desires are not necessarily those explicitly stated in the protasis of the hypothetical imperative. The protasis is about wanting to get the thing off, but the relevant desires may include wanting to get the thing off easily, wanting not to damage the head of the screw, and indefinitely many other things, even perhaps wanting to use the nearest screwdriver available when the speaker knows that this is a Phillips head one.

Instead of using the hypothetical imperative 'If you want . . .' the speaker, knowing that the addressee *does* want to get the thing off, could have said simply 'Use a Phillips head screwdriver'. Why should the addressee be motivated to comply with this imperative? Well, the speaker might have no legal authority

Why moral language?

over the addressee, but the addressee might simply want to please the speaker. Leaving such possibilities as these out of account, the addressee will want to comply with the imperative because of certain beliefs that he or she has about the speaker's own beliefs. The addressee will typically have good reasons to think that the speaker has good reasons to believe, or is in a good position to believe, certain factual propositions which are such that if the addressee believed them too the addressee's desire (to get the thing off) would be channelled into a desire to use a Phillips head screwdriver. Thus it may not be convenient, or there may not be time, or it may be hard to put felicitously into words, certain factual statements that could be used Zimmerman-like to canalize the addressee's desires. 'You ought to do X' (or for that matter 'Do X') hints at practically relevant factual knowledge.

It might be instructive here to compare this practical use of 'ought' with the epistemic and theoretical use of 'ought' in such a sentence as 'It ought to rain tomorrow' or 'The porridge ought to be cool by now'. Such sentences hint at reasons (for example the weather map or Newton's law of cooling) from which one could deduce (or at least show to be probable) the proposition 'It will rain tomorrow' or 'The porridge is cool'. One might argue, Zimmerman-like, that these 'ought' statements do no useful job: we could more concretely and effectively utter certain 'is' statements, such as 'There is a low pressure area to the west of us', or the statement of Newton's law of cooling, or whatever we think is behind our 'ought' statement. Sometimes, however, we justifiably assert something on the basis of reasons that we cannot easily drag into consciousness, though we know we have them. So we may know that a person ought to be here by now or that the porridge ought to be cool, even though we would have to scratch our heads a bit to say what our reasons were.

Sometimes an 'ought' statement hints not so much at reasons as at a rule. 'You ought to move this piece diagonally' hints at a rule of chess. Still, the rule by itself does not give a reason for action: what gives a reason for action is our desire to obey the rule, which can be canalized by the 'is' statement that it is a rule of chess that pieces of this sort move diagonally. (I am assuming that the piece in question is either a bishop or a pawn about to take another piece. If the piece were a queen or a king the

Why moral language?

'ought' would hint not at a rule of chess but at a maxim of tactics. In this case we could equally well persuade a player who wanted to win if we used a suitable tactical 'is' statement.)

Let us return to the moral case, in which, as I have said, 'You ought to do X' hints at practically relevant factual information. By a natural extension it may be taken as hinting not only at beliefs relevant to the addressee's desires, but also at beliefs relevant to the desires of other people or of society generally.[5] Now the addressee will have been conditioned in childhood to comply, other things being equal, with the wishes of his father and mother, his teachers, and so on, and indeed of people generally. Even if only for the sake of a quiet life, a person's belief that other people want him to do X will channel that person's desire to comply with other people's wishes into a desire to do X, other things being equal, or nearly equal. So the wishes of his mother, father, relations and friends, or of society generally, come in as facts to be taken into account in furthering his own desires. It is his desires, not theirs, that get canalized.

Usually the speaker will not have the time or energy to detail the 'is' circumstances relevant to the addressee's desires. Or, again, the addressee may not want to be bothered with possibly a long rigmarole. The utterance 'You ought to do X' simply indicates to the addressee that the speaker may know of factual propositions such that if the addressee were apprised of them they would canalize the addressee's desires into a desire to do X. And the addressee's being apprised of *this* fact about the speaker may itself result in the addressee's desires in fact being canalized into a desire to do X.

Why 'ought' language even so? Would it not be more honest or explicit if the speaker were simply to say 'It will help you get what you want if you do X'? (Perhaps, to deal with weakness of will, the fact that our desires may conflict, and so on, it would be preferable to modify 'what you desire' here to 'for what you have an over-riding desire', but I shall neglect this complication.) It is surely a 'conversational implicature'[6] of 'You ought to do X', not a part of what is actually asserted, that doing X will subserve the addressee's desires. When a 'right to life' advocate says 'You ought not to have an abortion' to a certain sort of feminist, he or she does not necessarily think that the feminist's actual desires will be satisfied by heeding the exhortation. Nevertheless the right-to-life advocate is not achieving anything by his or her 'ought' statement, except perhaps letting off steam and nailing his or her colours to the mast.

In trying to see a need for 'ought' language it will help to look at imperatives. Imperatives, even though given in a 'take it or leave it' spirit (i.e. not as the expression of legally authorized commands) have the advantage of brevity over factual want canalizing statements. 'Screw down top threaded race. . . . Set it hand tight, then back it off one quarter turn. Pile on washer, cable anchor mount, etc. and locknut. Check for play.' This quotation comes from *Richard's Bicycle Book*.[7] Obviously in a sequence of imperatives, 'Do A', 'Do B', 'Do C', 'Do D', say, it would be very awkward and verbose to put in clauses 'If you want X bring about D', 'if you want D bring about C', 'If you want C bring about B', 'If you want B bring about A', and in the quotation from *Richard's Bicycle Book* the matter is even more complicated. If we have a trusting addressee the use of simple imperatives saves a great deal of circumlocution that would be needed if we were to use explicit hypothetical imperatives, still more so if we suppose that the hypothetical imperatives are replaced by suitable 'is' statements, such as 'D causes X', 'C causes D', and so on. No doubt this function of saving circumlocution often accounts for the use of 'ought' statements too.

It seems, then, that in practical contexts 'You ought to do X' subserves much the same function as the 'is' statement 'Doing X will bring about what you want to happen'.

In making these observations I am not trying to give the meaning of the word 'ought'. I am not being reductionist, trying to *translate* 'ought' language into 'is' language. As I have remarked earlier I have learned from W.V. Quine to be suspicious of talk of meaning and of translation. I am here concerned with the pragmatics rather than with the semantics of moral language, and with Zimmerman's argument for the dispensability of moral language. I am trying to understand why we use 'ought' language at all. One reason might be for mystification, but I have here tried to suggest a more respectable reason: the avoidance of circumlocution.

Why moral language?

HYPOTHETICAL IMPERATIVES

What sort of an 'If . . .' clause do we have in an imperative like 'If you want to get the thing off, use a Phillips head screwdriver'? It does not seem to be analogous to the sort of 'If . . .' clause that can occur in what Kant would classify as a categorical imperative, such as 'If you have promised to do X, do X'.[8] It seems to be not a true protasis of a hypothetical but seems to be analogous to J.L. Austin's 'If you want biscuits there are some on the sideboard'.[9] In Austin's example the protasis states a condition of appropriately uttering the apodosis, not of the truth of the apodosis itself. The biscuits are on the sideboard whether you want them or not. Similarly the 'If . . .' clause in 'If you want X do A' expresses simply a condition for appropriately uttering the imperative 'Do A'.

If you want X it is appropriate for me to say 'Do A' if your doing A will bring about X. Hence if it is appropriate to say 'If you want X do A' it is also appropriate to say 'Doing A will bring about X'. For this reason John C. Harsanyi's and Philippa Foot's defences of morality as a system of hypothetical imperatives come very near to Zimmerman's nihilism, i.e. to proposing that we can do without 'ought' statements or imperatives.[10]

DESIRES

John McDowell has denied that 'the motivating power of all reasons derives from their including desires'.[11] He says that the facts surrounding a person's action may show the action as appearing to the agent in 'a favourable light'. But isn't something appearing in a favourable light the same as being wanted? McDowell concedes that we would no doubt credit a person who saw something in a favourable light as having an appropriate desire, say for his future happiness. This seems to be to admit that there *is* an appropriate desire, even though it may be, as McDowell goes on to contend, that the only *reason* for ascribing this desire is the reason that we cite. I take it that this reason would be that the person in question has certain beliefs. This seems to me to go no way to show that the reasons for actions need not include a desire. Our only reason for believing that a girder has metal fatigue may be the collapse of the girder, but this is not to deny that the fatigue is a real entity distinguishable from the collapse.[12] I thus find McDowell's argument puzzling, and so far see no conclusive objection to the Zimmerman-Foot position. McDowell's remarks about 'a favourable light' should presumably be seen in relation to his new, naturalistic form of intuitionism, but in the previous chapter I have found this view to be problematical.

The assumption that actions always have to be caused in part by a desire is very plausible. Consider a computer to navigate a pilotless aeroplane. Such a computer must contain an effector mechanism, a mechanism programmed to initiate action on the basis of data from the rest of the computer, unlike a computer that would merely give out the aeroplane's position on a tape. This necessity for action of duality of computer and effector is reflected in common sense psychology by the duality of belief and desire. It is true that we sometimes say that we do something because we ought, not because we want to, and indeed in opposition to our desires. This way of speaking conceals the fact that we must have a stronger desire to obey a set of conventional moral rules, or perhaps to act in accordance with an over-riding desire. These last desires get forgotten and we get the mistaken impression that we act from no desire at all. The situation is not helped when this easily forgotten desire gets called, as by Kant, 'will', or even 'reason'.

I am of course using 'desire' and 'to want' in a wide sense. As Davidson has said, 'It is not unnatural, in fact, to treat wanting as a genus including all pro attitudes as species'.[13] We must not allow post-Wittgensteinian analytical subtlety in making distinctions get in the way of smooth generalization when this seems warranted. (Cf. the traditional concept of *conation*, which is quite general.) I have also found that the view that moral persuasion always involves appeal to desires has sometimes been taken to imply psychological egoism or even psychological hedonism. This is a mistake. Desires can be as altruistic or even 'moral' as you like, as in the case of a desire to obey some system of precepts in which one has been indoctrinated. They can also be neither selfish nor altruistic nor 'moral', as in the case of what Bishop Butler called 'the particular passions'.[14] The idea that there can be action that does not proceed from a desire is perhaps

Why moral language?

facilitated in some cases by a certain ambiguity in the notions of 'reason' and 'motive' (reason or motive as cause as against reason or motive as justification). The fact that sometimes sentences about motives can be construed as sentences giving *justification* of action does not contradict the proposition that all actions have motives (desires) as causes.[15]

I am not contending of course that even a modified or streamlined version of the ordinary common-sense psychology of belief and desire will provide tight scientific explanations. But it is the best we can do at the moment, and provides some causal understanding of action. I take desires and beliefs to be postulated entities of common-sense (or near common-sense) psychology. Sometimes, though a person wants it to be the case that p, and believes that it will be the case that p only if he or she does A, he or she will nevertheless not do A. He or she may fail to do A because of incapacity, excitement, lethargy, or whatever. But in these cases failing to do A does not constitute an action, or if it does, as in the case of lethargy, we can point to another desire – in this case the desire not to exert oneself. Indeed it is enough for my purposes in this book if 'Wanting it to be the case that p' is a necessary (but not sufficient) condition of *intentionally* making it the case that p.

If ultimately our common-sense psychology is replaced by a radically different scientific psychology, in which explanation is directly related to the nervous system and its functional states, it is reasonable to suppose that (as in the case of the pilotless aeroplane with its computer plus effector mechanism) the belief-desire dichotomy will be represented in another guise. Talk of beliefs and desires will not of course be replaced by talk of anatomically separate components of the nervous system. Different functional states can be realized in shared components, as when a valve in a radio may constitute both an amplifier and a frequency changer. It should be conceded, however, that there will not be a close fit between the common-sense notions of belief and desire and the detailed information-flow scientific concepts that may replace them. This is because belief and desire are propositional attitudes, and the notion of 'proposition' is related to that of meaning (two sentences express the same proposition only if they are synonymous), and thus the notions of 'proposition' and of the propositional attitudes are indeterminate. Do

Why moral language?

'Dalton believed that atoms exist' and 'Dalton believed that indivisible particles exist' tell us about the same belief or not? There is no clear fact of the matter to be discussed here.

SOME NECESSARY QUALIFICATIONS

What about the case in which in a particular situation we are asking ourselves what we ought to do? We might put it as though it were a factual question: 'What do I most want to do in a case like this?' or perhaps 'What is my over-riding desire in a case like this?' We are reviewing all the facts pertinent to our case. We could be described as 'weighing reasons' for action. This seems mysterious. Is it the ascertaining of one's competing desires, and then acting on the desire that one decides is strongest? This would have to be motivated by a higher order desire to act on the strongest lower order desire. (This would seem to conflict with the phenomenon of *akrasia*, which suggests that our higher order desire may be to act from a *weaker* lower order desire, and to make this more likely in the future by doing things that inculcate habits that strengthen the weaker lower order desire, in the hope that it may come to be no longer weaker.) Another possibility is that the so-called weighing of reasons is merely ascertaining and reflecting on the various facts, thus causing the balance of our desires to alter. When equilibrium is attained this may trigger action or a resolution to act later.

In a discussion note Winston Nesbitt has argued against Philippa Foot's view that morality is a system of hypothetical imperatives, and hence by implication against Zimmerman's position.[16] Nesbitt claims that moral considerations give one reason to act no matter what one's interests and desires happen to be. He also states that a person has reason to do some action only if it would promote some end that he or she desires. It is not clear from the discussion note how he reconciles these two apparently contrary propositions, but he has kindly sent me Chapters 10 and 11 of his PhD thesis[17] in which he brilliantly argues so as to reconcile these apparent contraries.

Nesbitt's argument depends on the notion of co-operation to attain some end, and I have been helped to see the importance of Nesbitt's argument by reading Donald Regan's impressive book

Why moral language?

Utilitarianism and Co-operation.[18] In what follows I shall be very much indebted to Nesbitt's views, but I shall all the same try to fit them as far as possible into a Zimmerman-like or Foot-like framework.

Suppose that a number of people have the possibility of co-operating to achieve some commonly desired end E. This end E will be achieved if nearly all of these people do co-operate. Any individual might reason as follows: 'If I do not co-operate I can attain some other end F. If most others co-operate E will be attained anyway and as a bonus I shall attain F. So in this case I will get more of what I want if I do not co-operate. On the other hand if not enough other persons do co-operate it is almost certain that my own co-operation would not tip the balance so as to do any good, and so once more I will get more of what I want if I forget about E, and as a non-co-operator aim simply for F. So in either case the overwhelming probability is that I would do best by not co-operating.' Thus I might excuse myself from the tedium of attending a (potentially large) meeting. If lots of people go a quorum will be achieved and I am not needed. If not many go there is no quorum even if I go too. So once more I am not needed.

If everyone reasons in this individualistic fashion outcome E is not going to be achieved. Yet E may be very much wanted by everyone and so in a sense it seems irrational for people to argue in this fashion. There seems to be a rationality in co-operating. We can look at this in terms of a group of people constituting a super-personal agent whose rationality may exceed that of a mere aggregate of individuals. There need be nothing mysterious or anti-mechanist about this.[19] After all, different parts of one person's brain co-operate with one another. It is not difficult to think of rationality as pertaining also to a spatially scattered 'super-brain' (group of brains), and of the multiple actions of the individuals in a group as adding up to constitute a single action of the group as a whole. Each member of the group would *de facto* have a desire to co-operate in general. John Kilcullen has pointed out to me that J.S. Mill's apparently paradoxical remark that a utilitarian must desire virtue for its own sake[20] may be understood as something like what I have just said about the necessity for a desire simply to co-operate.[21] Nesbitt sees the need for co-operation as explaining the categorical imperative that he holds to be characteristic of morality. Morality, he holds, enables individuals to attain co-operatively certain ends (in Hobbesian terms 'peace', though among certain groups other ends may come into it, such as the general promotion of happiness, as for example is shown by the recent interest in extending our moral concern to animals). They desire these ends, but could not attain them if they acted solely on these desires. Thus Nesbitt reconciles his two contrary propositions.

It still seems to me that there is no need for the moral 'ought'. People will not co-operate unless they *want* to co-operate.[22] Wanting the ends that co-operation will enable us to achieve is not sufficient, for the reasons given two paragraphs back. One could say to a Hobbesian, for example, 'You want to co-operate with others in attaining peace: peace is attained by most people behaving in accordance with the moral practices of your society. These include usually keeping promises, telling the truth, and so on. So co-operating to achieve peace implies usually telling the truth, keeping promises, etc.' These are all 'is' statements. It is not clear that we need an 'ought' statement, a categorical imperative. Or, again, a society of utilitarians, who had implanted in them a desire to co-operate, might be induced to do so by the 'is' statement that co-operating in certain ways will maximize the general happiness.

Of course we must *want* to co-operate. We must, as Nesbitt puts it, see ourselves as part of a group, not as an individual. Where does the desire to co-operate come from? No doubt mainly from social conditioning, but it is also plausible that a propensity in this direction is useful enough to have evolved by natural selection. In this social conditioning the language of 'ought' and of imperatives is very convenient. In so far as parents and teachers have a sort of quasi-legal authority this use of 'ought' and of imperatives is rather like the military one, though in principle it could be dispensed with in terms of such 'is' statements as 'If you do this I shall smack you, send you to bed, get upset, or whatever'. Since imperatives can probably be learned before the word 'if' can be learned, the usefulness of imperatives is plain. (One says 'sit' to a dog, but hardly 'If . . .'!)

My own inclination therefore is to try to accommodate Nesbitt's insights to a Zimmerman-like or Foot-like position. Nesbitt's way (to which in this short discussion I have necessarily

Why moral language?

done but imperfect justice) of reconciling the categorical imperative with a morality based on our desires is certainly worth further thought. We must also not forget that many moral decisions do not require co-operation: a man all alone on a river bank will out of benevolence dive in to rescue a drowning man. Zimmerman's judge can sentence the prisoner without having to co-operate with other judges. And so on. In such cases we can appeal to an agent's desires without having to include an appeal to a desire on the part of the agent to co-operate with other agents.

IV

CONSIDERATIONS ABOUT THE SEMANTICS OF 'OUGHT'

CONTEXT-DEPENDENCE OF 'OUGHT'

In the previous chapter we were concerned with the pragmatics of 'ought', as it is used in certain central contexts. But what about the *semantics* of 'ought'? I shall not be able to give a full treatment of this matter (or, in the next chapter, of the semantics of 'good'), because it impinges on certain fundamental questions which are still controversial among philosophers of language. Nevertheless certain issues are perhaps becoming clearer.

It seems to be clear that the word 'ought' is a very contextually related one. Thus we have the moral 'ought' as in 'Jim ought to keep his promise to Mary', a slightly immoral one, as in 'John ought to put his money on such and such a horse' (even though he has promised his wife to give up gambling), a technical 'ought', as in the statement that if a burglar wants to blow up a certain safe he ought to use gelignite, and an epistemic 'ought', as in 'it ought to rain tomorrow'. The strong context-dependence of 'ought' can be illustrated by the sentence 'Jones ought to have arrived by now'. According to the context this could be a moral 'ought', or it might be an epistemic 'ought'. Not all of these different examples of 'ought' should lead us to talk of different senses of the word. As explained in Chapter 1, I am trying to avoid use of the notion of meaning as much as possible, since I believe that Quinean considerations make it suspect. Nevertheless later in this chapter I shall refer to three senses of 'ought', where purely syntactical considerations make this legitimate. Mere context-relatedness should not lead us to talk of differences of meaning. This is most obvious in the extreme context-relatedness of indexicals. 'I will go to London' said by person P at time t is true if and only if P goes (tenseless) to London later than t. What is said depends on P and t but it would be wrong to say that the sentence 'I will go to London' differs in meaning when said by different persons and at different times. Again subjunctive conditionals are context-dependent since they refer to what follows from what according to certain contextually understood background information. Yet we should not talk of different senses of 'if it had been the case that', for example.

FITTINGNESS

I want to begin by canvassing an illuminating but nevertheless also misleading account of 'ought', which as applied to moral contexts goes back to the eighteenth century and Samuel Clarke's notion of 'fitness'.[1] In more recent times this sort of account was put forward, again for moral contexts, by C.D. Broad who in his *Five Types of Ethical Theory* elucidated rightness as fittingness to a situation, and by Sir David Ross in his *Foundations of Ethics*.[2] I should stress that I should reject many of the things that these writers say about this relation, such as that it is unanalysable and known by supersensible intuition.

In its most general form the account is that the word 'ought' has something to do with a relation between something or other and a situation. In most of the examples I have mentioned it is tempting to say that the relation is between an act and a situation. In the case of 'Jim ought to keep his promise to Mary' the fittingness will be that of his act being in accordance with certain moral rules which apply in the situation in which he finds himself. (What these rules are will also depend on the context. For example, a certain sort of deontologist, and probably also the ordinary non-philosophical person in the street, may point simply to the rule 'keep promises', whereas an act utilitarian will point to the rule of maximizing happiness and to the particular situation in which the rule must be applied.) In the case of 'John ought to put his money on such and such a horse' the fittingness

Considerations about the semantics of 'ought'

that is contextually implied is that of a fittingness of his act of gambling to the probabilities of various performances and the odds given for them. In the case of the burglar the fittingness that is implied is the technological fittingness of an act of using gelignite to the situation of being confronted by a locked safe, given the purposes of the burglar. The epistemic 'ought' does not fit the account, since any fittingness implied is not that of an act to a situation, but if the account were generalized a bit it could be made to fit, since there still seems to be an implied fittingness of some sort, perhaps that of a proposition to our current beliefs.

This account of 'ought' as signifying fittingness does therefore point the way to a unified treatment of the word 'ought', as it occurs in both moral and non-moral contexts. Unfortunately it will not do as it stands. Let A be the (possible) act of Jim keeping his promise to Mary in situation S. Unfortunately Jim may not do what he ought. So there may not be an act A to stand in a relation to S.

Though regrettably the act of Jim's keeping his promise to Mary may not exist, perhaps we can construe the 'ought' as signifying an (at least) three-way relation btween Jim, the property of keeping a promise to Mary, and the situation S. This is to assume that the world contains *properties*, but if we reject properties in our ontology, the job can be done by talking of predicates in the English language instead. Situations are suspect entities too. In the *Tractatus* Wittgenstein said that the world consists of facts and not of things, whereas we ought to say that it consists of things and not of facts.[3] Situations seem to be in the same boat as facts. I shall return to this matter in Chapter 6.

Perhaps, then, we should say that 'Jim ought to keep his promise to Mary' has the form 'Jim ought true of himself "... keep his promise to Mary" '. The expression 'ought true of himself' would be thought of as expressing a triadic relation between Jim, the property of keeping his promise to Mary, and a time. (Or a 4-adic relation between Jim, the English predicate 'keeps his promise to Mary', a time, and because there are many Marys, a context. Context will also be required to distinguish between a moral interpretation and, say, an epistemic one.)

The account still needs modification, because of the intensionality of 'keeps his promise to Mary'. Presumably the property of keeping his promise to Mary is not the same as that of keeping

Considerations about the semantics of 'ought'

his promise to the girl who won the hundred metre sprint (and quite obviously the English expressions are different). Yet if Jim ought to keep his promise to Mary he ought to keep it to the girl who won the hundred metre sprint, given that Mary won the hundred metre sprint. I shall deal with this problem on page 76. Or we could use a different notation and stipulate that if 'Ought (Jim, t, Pr)' is true, then 'Ought (Jim, t, Pr^*)' is true too, if Pr^* is extensionally equivalent to Pr. Thus '... keeps his promise to Mary' is extensionally equivalent to '... keeps his promise to the girl who won the hundred metre sprint' if Mary = the girl who won the hundred metre sprint. (I have inserted the time variable 't' which denotes an instant or perhaps a vaguely specified interval of time, since what may be an appropriate action at one time may not be so at others and an action is something that occurs at an instant on the world line in space-time of a person's body.)

DEONTIC LOGIC

Without going into this approach in further detail, I want to say that the idea of treating 'ought' as some sort of relational predicate contrasts with the approach found in deontic logic, in which 'ought' is treated as a modal operator. In deontic logic the 'ought' is brought out to the front of the sentence and 'Jim ought to keep his promise to Mary' is treated as of the form 'It ought to be the case that Jim keeps his promise to Mary'. But now suppose that Mary is the girl who was seduced by the man next door. Then if Jim ought to keep his promise to Mary he ought to keep his promise to the girl who was seduced by the man next door. But clearly it ought not to be the case that Jim keeps his promise to the girl who was seduced, because this implies that it ought to be the case that the girl was seduced. (If $O(p \& q)$ then Oq.) (This is a variant of the well-known Good Samaritan paradox in deontic logic – if someone ought to succour the man who fell among thieves, it would seem to follow, given the approach in deontic logic of treating 'ought' as a modal operator, that it ought to be the case that a man fell among thieves.)

Similarly for the technological 'ought'. Suppose we say that the burglar ought to use a certain piece of gelignite. The piece of gelignite that will do the job may be expensive. So he ought to use expensive gelignite. Nevertheless the burglar could consistently deny that it ought to be the case that the gelignite is expensive.

Treating the 'ought' as a modal operator naturally goes with a possible worlds semantics: what we ought to do is what we would do in a deontically perfect world. In the moral case this would be a world in which all promises were kept, no thieves existed, no girls were seduced, and so on. In the burglar's technologically perfect world he (or his counterpart in that world) would use effective and inexpensive explosives. And yet we want to say that John ought to keep his promise to the girl who was seduced by the man next door, that the Samaritan ought to succour the man who fell among thieves, and we may also agree, from a technological though not from a moral point of view, that the burglar ought to use effective though expensive explosive.

There are other paradoxes that present the same sort of problem for deontic logic as does the Good Samaritan paradox. One way of dealing with the situation would be that of Hector-Neri Castañeda, who has given a unified treatment of the deontic paradoxes.[4] This would be to modify the rules of inference so as to block the inference, at least in the paradox-producing types of case, of Oq from $O(p \& q)$. Because I am not clear about the semantical problems that would be involved here, I prefer a different approach, that of Bruce Vermazen, who concludes that the moral of the deontic paradoxes is that the practical 'ought' is not a modal 'ought': the 'ought' cannot be brought out to the front of the sentence.[5]

Thus we are not using the practical 'ought' when we say 'It ought to be the case that there is no pain in the universe'. If we say this we are saying that in the best of all possible universes there exists no pain. It is tempting to elucidate this deontic modality in terms of possible worlds (whether we take this locution quite literally or not) just as possible worlds semantics fits naturally with the alethic modality 'It is necessary that'. Just as 'it is possible that' is interchangeable with 'it is not the case that it is necessarily the case that it is not the case that' ($Mp \equiv {\sim}L {\sim}p$), so we might introduce an operator P such that Pp is eqivalent to 'It is not the case that it ought not to be the case that' ($Pp \equiv {\sim}O{\sim}p$), but I think it is a bit misleading to translate

'P*p*' as 'It is *permissible* that *p*'. 'Permissible' goes with the practical 'ought', not with the 'ought' that fits the modal semantics, which Vermazen calls 'the ideal "ought" '. Eric Dayton has similarly suggested that this 'ought' expresses the notion, not of obligation but of 'subjective betterness'.[6] In thus separating the 'ought' of so-called deontic logic from the practical 'ought' he is in agreement with Vermazen's view.

THREE SENSES OF 'OUGHT'

In fact Vermazen wants to distinguish *three* senses of 'ought'. Besides the ideal and the practical 'ought's there is the epistemic 'ought'. Suppose that we are at a meeting and Professor Smith says 'Professor Jones ought to be here in about ten minutes'. Professor Smith is a tolerant man and we do not take him, in the context, as criticizing Jones's tardiness from the point of view of morality, etiquette, or whatever else. We take his 'ought' as what I have referred to as the epistemic 'ought'. Perhaps ten minutes earlier Smith had driven in his car past Jones at a spot about a mile from the meeting place, and had noticed Jones walking in the right direction at three miles per hour.

The statement that Jones ought to be here in ten minutes' time could be paraphrased by saying that the statement that Jones will be here in ten minutes' time is warranted by the best available evidence.[7] Professor Robinson might deny Smith's statement by saying 'No, I don't think that Jones ought to be here in ten minutes' time. He always calls in at his room in the university so as to collect his papers for the meeting, and he generally has his papers in such a mess that it takes him about fifteen minutes to find the right ones.' Robinson is pointing out that the statement that Jones will be here in ten minutes' time is not, after all, warranted by the best available evidence. If one interpreted this by 'possible worlds' talk (though I am not sure that we should do so) we could say that 'Jones ought to be here in ten minutes' is true if 'Jones is here in ten minutes' is true in all possible worlds epistemically (not just logically) consistent with the available evidence. More difficult to deal with are such sentences as 'Jones ought to have been here by now', where the available evidence includes the patently obvious fact that Jones is *not* here: we have to discount this evidence and other evidence that warrants it. This leads us into familiar problems of the semantics of counterfactual conditionals, and I shall not attempt to deal with these here.[8]

Suppose that a member of the committee, Brown, volunteers the information that he has just discovered that Jones is the president of the university mountaineering society. If this fact is added as an extra premiss to 'Jones ought to be here in about ten minutes', it follows logically that the president of the university mountaineering society ought to be here in about ten minutes. This and other differences of logical behaviour, depending on the underlying grammar, enable us to distinguish the 'ought' here as having a different sense from the 'ought' of subjective betterness. Suppose someone were to say that it ought to be the case that a certain old English cricketer should be the Pope. With the additional information that this cricketer injured his hand in such and such a match, we cannot deduce that it ought to be the case that the man who injured his hand in this match be the Pope. We might prefer a world in which the cricketer (or rather his counterpart in that world) was both Pope and had never hurt his hand.

These cases show that a certain referential transparency is characteristic of the epistemic 'ought' which does not exist in the case of the 'ought' of subjective betterness. However the epistemic 'ought' is not referentially transparent in the full sense, since transparency in question depends on it being warranted by the best available evidence that the identity statement in question holds. I do not think that we ought to say that the president of the university mountaineering club ought to be here in ten minutes if we were not warranted in believing that Jones and the president of the university mountaineering club were identical. On the other hand, if I ought to keep my promises to Mary, then, if Mary is the girl who won the hundred metre sprint, it follows, *tout court* and whether or not I am warranted in believing that Mary is the girl who won the hundred metre sprint, that I ought to keep my promise to the girl who won the hundred metre sprint. Similarly suppose that a certain burglar ought to use gelignite to open a certain safe. Suppose also that it happens to be the case that the burglar in question is the only person who was in Trafalgar Square at 2.00 a.m. on 1st April 1980. It then follows that the only person who was in Trafalgar Square at 2.00 a.m. on 1st April 1980 ought to use gelignite to open the safe. The practical 'ought' belongs naturally in completely referentially transparent contexts.

Thus, following Vermazen, we can distinguish three main senses of 'ought'. The differences between them are differences in formal logic and so survive the reluctance to distinguish 'senses' that goes with suspicion of the analytic-synthetic distinction, and the threefold distinction goes naturally with a recognition of the context-dependence of 'ought' statements. By contrast the difference between the 'ought' of 'I ought to keep my promise to Mary' and the 'ought' of 'The burglar ought to use gelignite' is not a difference of sense or meaning. We have one sense but the truth conditions of the two just-mentioned sentences differ partly in virtue of the difference between the contexts of these sentences.

Lack of attention to context-dependence, and a less critical attitude to the concept of 'meaning', has led philosophers to distinguish different 'senses' of 'ought', 'good' and so on, even when there are no quasi-grammatical or formally logical criteria such as those that led Vermazen to distinguish his three senses. In particular it has been common to distinguish 'ought' and 'good' in moral senses from 'ought' and 'good' in non-moral senses. Thus even within the practical 'ought', philosophers have commonly distinguished between 'morally ought' and a purely instrumental 'ought', so that it would be held that when we say that the burglar ought to use gelignite we are using 'ought' in a non-moral sense. In an important book Roger Wertheimer has argued against this 'doctrine of moral senses', as he calls it.[9] As Vermazen has pointed out in a review of Wertheimer's book, context-dependence of sentences in which a word occurs does not make the word ambiguous.[10] Thus Vermazen's position lies between that of moral philosophers, such as Moore and Ross, who distinguish too many senses, without grammatical or quasi-grammatical warrant for so doing, and Wertheimer who distinguishes only one sense. As Vermazen suggests in his review this lays Wertheimer open to paradoxes such as that of the Good Samaritan.

If this is right then we should follow Vermazen and distinguish (at least) three senses of 'ought': (1) the 'ideal' ought (the 'ought' of subjective betterness); (2) the epistemic 'ought'; and (3) the practical 'ought'. We should resist the temptation, however to subdivide (3) and talk of moral and non-moral senses of 'ought'. What we have are moral and non-moral contexts, which affect the illocutionary force of a single 'ought'. There is, however, the question, put to me by Helen Nissenbaum, as to how one distinguishes moral and non-moral contexts. It would of course be circular to say that the context of 'ought' is moral or non-moral according to whether 'ought' is used with moral or non-moral illocutionary force. In fact if we reject the view that there are moral and non-moral senses of the practical 'ought' it is not very important how finely we distinguish moral and non-moral contexts. There is in some cases a clear difference in the sort of context we have in mind: consider 'Even burglars ought to keep their promises' and 'Burglars ought to use gelignite in order to get inside safes'. In the former the context is not one of special concern for the special purposes of burglars as such, whereas in the former the context does imply concern for these special purposes and excludes wider human concerns. We can understand this without drawing a sharp line between the moral and the non-moral contexts. The case was different with those who, like Moore and Ross, believed in *a priori* synthetic moral intuitions. They had to hold, however implausibly, that there were different senses of the practical 'ought', since it would be implausible to say that any synthetic *a priori* intuitions come into the judgment that a burglar ought to use gelignite, or that in cricket a batsman ought to keep his bat straight.

THE PRACTICAL 'OUGHT'

Looking at the practical 'ought', then, we see that it is not a modal 'ought', as is the ideal 'ought'. Thus the expression I mentioned on p. 66 above, 'ought true of himself' is a predicate, not an operator.

Should we then say that in the case of the practical 'ought' we are concerned with a relation between an agent and an English expression? In line with what was said on p. 66 it should perhaps be concerned with a relation between a person, a predicate expression, a sequence of individuals and (we should now add) a time, since it may be the case that Jim ought to keep his promise to Mary at t and yet not keep it at some other time.

It may be objected that when philosophers discuss the word 'ought' they do not mean to refer specifically to the English language. Still, we could adopt a general rule that 'ought' refers to the English language, 'soll' refers to the German language, 'doit' refers to the French language, and so on. Or we could go linguistically neutral and talk of a relation between an agent and a property (not an English or other predicate). Any unclarity, such as Quine has drawn attention to, in the notion of a property, trades off with a comparable unclarity in the notions of translation and of what constitutes a single language. In any case it need not be supposed that the language of ethical discourse can be carried out with completely clear concepts. I shall choose the alternative of discussing predicates in the English language. We can now relate this to the semantics of the English language. I shall make use of Vermazen's semantic theory of the practical 'ought'.

Vermazen wants to account for various sorts of inference that we can make from a sentence of the form 'Ought (a, t, F)' where F is a predicate corresponding to an action type. Thus F might be 'keeps his promise to Mary'. (I use Roman 'F', not italic 'F', to indicate that 'F' is not a dummy predicate but a dummy name of a predicate.) Vermazen's theory in fact does it in a different way, but another way to allow for the deduction of 'Jim keeps his promise to the girl who won the hundred metre sprint' from 'Jim keeps his promise to Mary' and 'Mary is the girl who won the hundred metre sprint' and the like would be to replace F by an ordered pair $<F^*, s>$ where F^* might be 'keeps his promise' and s might be $<$John, Mary$>$. Or in the case of 'John introduces Tom to Mary', it might be $<$'introduces $x\ y\ z$', $<$John, Tom, Mary$>>$. For perspicuity I have here replaced the predicate 'introduces' by the open sentence 'introduces $x\ y\ z$' ('x introduces y to z') where the sequence of variables $<$'x', 'y', 'z'$>$ matches up with the sequence of persons $<$John, Tom, Mary$>$. And of course if Tom is the Prime Minister and Mary is the girl who won the hundred metre sprint, then $<$John, Tom, Mary$>$ = $<$John, the Prime Minister, the girl who won the hundred metre sprint$>$.

The truth conditions of 'Ought (a, t, F)' will depend on context. They may be conduciveness to some end, conformity

Considerations about the semantics of 'ought'

with some social rule, the action in question being approved by the speaker, and so on. This raises all sorts of issues that will have to wait for Chapter 6. But given the truth conditions of 'Ought (*a*, *t* F)' (here 'ought' is a triadic predicate) Vermazen wants to account semantically for various types of inference. Thus suppose that Ought (*a*, *t*, F) where F is 'makes an omelette' and in order to make an omelette it is causally necessary to break eggs, then 'Ought (*a*, *t*, "break eggs")' must also be true. Again, one cannot waltz without dancing, because waltzing is a species of dancing. We can therefore deduce from 'Ought (*a*, *t*, "waltz")' and 'Waltzing is dancing' the sentence 'Ought (*a*, *t*, "dances")'. Vermazen considers other types of case but these two are enough to give the general idea. In order to account for inferences of the various sorts Vermazen introduces the notion of a Plan. The capital 'P' indicates that Vermazen's notion of a Plan is more specialized than is the ordinary notion of a 'plan' (small 'p'). Vermazen defines a Plan as an ordered triple <*a*, *t*, P> where *a* is an agent, *t* a time, and *P* a consistent set of open sentences in which the only gap (or unbound variable) in an open sentence that is not negated occupies the place which could be filled by the name of an agent. Vermazen gives the examples '*x* walks' '*x* eats something', '*x* buys the drinks'. The theory specifies the open sentences that can be members of *P* and how a Plan differs from a plan (small 'p').

In effect a Plan specifies what must be done in order to accomplish the end of an action. (In the moral case this might be thought to legislate for a teleological form of ethics, such as utilitarianism, but this is not so, because in deontological ethics the end could be simply to comply with the moral law.) Thus if the end of the action is to make an omelette (Vermazen's example) then '. . . breaks an egg' would be one of the action predicates in the Plan, but '. . . uses butter' will not be, because an alternative would be '. . . uses margarine'. Perhaps 'uses butter or uses margarine' will be in the Plan. Here the end of the action was taken to be to make an omelette: equally it could be to feed one's wife. Here '. . . make an omelette' might answer to a subordinate end in the Plan, but only if making an omelette was the only possible way of feeding one's wife, if, for example there was some medical reason why she could eat only omelettes.

Thus a Plan differs from a plan. Putting the matter informally, it could be part of one's plan to use butter, but not part of the relevant Plan. Some readers may worry about time order. The set P is not a sequence of predicates (or action types). Does it matter that jumping out of the window and then shouting may produce a relevantly different result from shouting and then jumping out of the window? Either it does or it does not produce a relevantly different result. If it does then only one of the two action types in question (the two being A-ing and then B-ing and B-ing and then A-ing, respectively) will be in the Plan. If it does not then only the disjunction of the two (A-ing and then B-ing or B-ing and then A-ing) is in the Plan. So P can still be a set, not a sequence.

This elucidation of an 'ought' statement in terms of a Plan explains various ways in which one 'ought' statement, together with a suitable minor premiss, may imply another 'ought' statement. Thus, to use the Vermazen example again, 'I ought to make an omelette' together with 'It is impossible to make an omelette without breaking eggs' implies 'I ought to break eggs'. Here the minor premiss is one of physical necessity. Sometimes the minor premiss will not be a statement of physical necessity but will be one of identity. Brutus stabs Caesar, and thereby kills Caesar. Donald Davidson has argued that there are not two actions here, a stabbing and a killing.[11] There is one action that can be alternatively described as a stabbing and as a killing. Of course not all stabbings are killings and not all killings are stabbings, but this particular stabbing was the very same action as this particular killing. There are lawlike propositions that imply that all actions of making an omelette are actions of breaking an egg or eggs. By contrast not all actions of making an omelette are actions of using butter, though they may (by physical necessity) perhaps all be actions of using butter or margarine. Again (perhaps by something stronger than physical necessity) all waltzing is dancing.[12] That is every action of waltzing is identical with some action of dancing.

Here there are two sorts of impossibility, the impossibility of making omelettes without breaking eggs, and the impossibility of waltzing without dancing. In the former case, breaking eggs is a physically necessary condition of making an omelette, and in the latter case waltzing is a species of dancing. There are other sorts of necessary condition discussed by Vermazen, such as failing to do something, and doing a part of a continuous process (e.g. to paint a wall you have to paint a part of it).

A Plan then gives a specification of necessary conditions, by means of re-descriptions of the action (or part of the action) in question. Then Vermazen explains the various deductions we can make of 'Tom ought to break eggs' from 'Tom ought to make omelettes', and 'Tom ought to dance' from 'Tom ought to waltz'. According to Vermazen's theory 'Ought (a, t, G)' is deducible from 'Ought (a, t, F)' if F specifies the 'end' in the Plan and G is a predicate in the set of predicates P in the Plan $<a, t, P>$, and more generally, if F occurs as specifying a subordinate end and G comes later in the recursion whereby the set P is generated. It is important to note that the agent need not be aware of the Plan or have any neurological representation of it. Suppose that the agent ought to get the plane to Sydney. Then if the plane leaves at 8.15 a.m. he ought to be at the airport before 8.00 a.m. However he may not know that the plane leaves at 8.15 a.m. and so will not know that he ought to be at the airport before 8.00 a.m. Similarly he may know that he ought to keep his promise to Mary, but not know that he ought to keep his promise to the girl who won the hundred metre sprint, being unaware of the identity of Mary and the girl who won the hundred metre sprint. The extensionality of 'ought' contexts is important for the understanding of Vermazen's concept of a Plan. Of course if an agent does plan (small 'p') to do what he ought, and if his plan is a good one, then in this case he will both be aware of his plan and the plan will be a further specification of the relevant Plan. We can account for our ability to deduce 'I ought to keep my promise to the girl who won the hundred metre sprint' from 'I ought to keep my promise to Mary' and 'Mary is (identical with) the girl who won the hundred metre sprint'. This is because Vermazen's specification of what it is to be a Plan (which I have not given in detail) implies or contains the proviso that if F is in a Plan and G is like F except for containing a co-extensive singular term, then G is in the Plan. Similarly from (1) 'We ought to buy the drinks' and (2) 'The drinks are Lucrezia Borgia's best poisons' we can deduce (3) 'We ought to buy Lucrezia Borgia's best poisons'. (If we reject (3) and accept (2) we may reconsider (1)!)

For it to be the case that an agent a ought (practically) to do an action A at time t, is for the corresponding predicate describing A to belong to the set P in a Plan of which a and t are the first two members. (Because of the difference between a Plan and a plan several actions can correspond to one and only one Plan.) Thus one can think of the practical 'ought' as expressing a relation between an agent, a time and a set of predicates. 'Ought' is not a modal operator. Of course one may assert that someone ought to do an action without knowing all the details of the appropriate Plan. One must of course know that the predicate that is made true by the agent accomplishing the end of the action is in the Plan, but one need not know that waltzing is dancing or that one cannot make omelettes without breaking eggs. The minor premisses 'Waltzing is dancing' and 'If you make an omelette it is physically necessary that you break an egg' include part of the information about what predicates are in the Plan, and they each legitimize the inferences from 'If you ought to waltz you ought to dance' and 'If you ought to make an omelette you ought to break an egg' respectively.

I have just spoken of 'the end of the action'. This must be contextually understood. In the case of the hypothetical imperative we have 'If you want to do X you ought to do Y'. Here the 'You ought to do X' is a practical 'ought' concerned with achieving the end of conforming to 'do X'. The agent may not in fact have this end: he may not want to do X. In the previous chapter I have suggested that 'If you want to do X do Y' is not a true hypothetical but is analogous to J.L. Austin's example 'If you want biscuits there are some on the sideboard'. This does not imply that if there are no biscuits on the sideboard you do not want biscuits. The supposition behind the 'If you want biscuits' is not a condition of there being biscuits on the sideboard but only of the pragmatic appropriateness of saying that there are biscuits. In saying 'If you want X do Y' I am saying that 'Do Y' is the appropriate imperative to give to you on the supposition that you want to conform to the imperative 'Bring about Y'. Equally we could say 'If you want X, you ought to do Y'. The 'If . . .' clause enables one to pick out the appropriate Plan for assessing the truth conditions of the clause 'You ought to do Y'. According to context the conjectured desire may be to obey conventional moral rules, to maximize the general happiness, or one's own happiness, to open a safe, to mend a bicycle, and so on.

In the previous chapter I suggested that there is no point in simply saying 'Do X' or 'You ought to do 'X' if the person you are addressing has no desire to obey your imperative or to do what you say he ought to do. This ties up with other suggestions that I made in that chapter: the practical 'ought' corresponds to a hypothetical imperative. We can now say that the 'ought' relates to a Plan fitting to the supposed desires of the agent. The moral 'ought' is relative to a desire to obey certain moral rules or a moral principle or more directly for the end or ends specified in such a principle. As was noted in the previous chapter, it may depend on a desire simply to co-operate in achieving some end, and the so-called categorical imperative could be interpreted as a hypothetical imperative referring to the supposed desire to co-operate. Such an independent desire to co-operate is readily explicable in terms of social conditioning, and it may well have a genetic source too. The advantages of co-operation were noted in the previous chapter.

Thus in the second person 'ought' statement we address ourselves, in the manner discussed in the previous chapter, to the desires of the agent: the Plan we have in mind will correspond to certain of these desires (perhaps just the desire to obey the conventional moral rules of the society). Of course, we often use third person 'ought' statements, as when we say that someone did or did not do what he ought. Sometimes the pragmatics of this may be (at least in part) persuasion of the person the 'ought' statement is about, as when a book reviewer writes that the author should not have said something, knowing that the author will be one of those who will read the review. Sometimes, again, persuasion may be aimed at third parties. Suppose that a father is watching a cricket match in the company of his young son. The father may say 'The batsman ought not to have played that sort of stroke', where the intention is to prevent his son from playing that sort of stroke when he plays himself. Sometimes the pragmatics will work both ways, as when the book reviewer says that the author of the book in question ought not to have said something or other, hoping to persuade both the author of the book and also other persons who might be tempted to say something similar themselves.

Vermazen's notion of a Plan incorporates the notion of an 'end' in a very wide way. It is not committed to the view that a person's ethics must be 'teleological'. A person's end might simply be compliance with various rules, or to maximize such compliance in some way or other if there is conflict of rules in particular cases. It covers all cases of the practical 'ought', not just the 'moral' one. It seems also to cover the distinction that some philosophers have made between 'subjective' and 'objective' rightness. Vermazen's semantic theory nicely elucidates the notion of 'ought' as signifying fittingness, which I discussed at the beginning of this chapter. Reverting to this way of talking for the moment, we can say that a Plan might fit the objective situation. On the other hand we could construct a parallel theory in which a Plan might fit our beliefs about the situation. There are various ways in which this might happen, but I wish to fasten here on a distinction which is made in utilitarian ethics. Thus a utilitarian might say that what an agent ought to do is maximize utility (pleasure, happiness or whatever). On the other hand, there is the consideration that the agent does not know for certain what the effects of his or her action will be. What he or she should do is to maximize expected utility. Expected utility is got by summing the products of the values of possible outcomes and their probabilities. To maximize expected utility must be clearly distinguished from probably maximizing utility.

Suppose that someone holds that driving at excessive speed from Melbourne to Sydney will probably maximize utility: the driver will *probably* not crash and will get to arrive in Sydney at the time he wants to. On the other hand there is a smaller and not negligible probability that he or she will not reach Sydney alive and will also cause death and injury to other motorists as well. So a good utilitarian (and no doubt a good non-utilitarian too) will want to do what will maximize expected utility. He or she will want to maximize the sum of the products of the probabilities and the values of the various possible effects of his action. Since the effects of a crash would be so bad, the product of the relatively small probability of a crash with the negative value of the effects of the crash will outweigh the product of the greater probability of not having a crash and the positive value of arriving in Sydney on time. Thus a utilitarian may say not 'Do what will probably maximize utility' but 'Do what will maximize the expected utility'. This subjective sort of 'ought' can easily be accommodated by Vermazen's semantics. Here the end specified in the appropriate Plan is not that of maximizing utility, or even of probably maximizing utility, but is that of maximizing expected utility. Similar considerations apply even within deontological ethics. An agent may want to do that action which maximizes compliance with moral rules, which may conflict in the situation with which he or she is confronted, but he or she may have to depend on various probabilities of so complying. (He or she may want to keep a promise to return a book, but not have complete faith in the country's postal service, so that he or she will give a probability of less than one to his action actually being one of keeping his promise.)

CONFLICTS OF OBLIGATION

As was indicated in the previous paragraph, though in a different context, traditional moral thinking, as elucidated by (say) Sir David Ross, is often done in terms not of 'ought' but of conflicting obligations. Ross introduced the term '*prima facie* duty', though he acknowledged that this is misleading.[13] Thus a man may say that he is obliged to bring about some end because he has promised to do so, but obliged not to do so because he can bring about the end only by telling a lie. If there are no relevant considerations he will try to weigh up the strength of the obligation to keep the promise against the strength of the obligation to tell a lie. This may suggest some sort of exercise of *a priori* synthetic intuitions, but because of the naturalistic metaphysics and epistemology I have advocated as a presupposition of the treatment of meta-ethics in this book, I would suggest that this 'weighing up' would be a letting of feelings towards promise keeping and truth telling come to a stable state in the light of contemplation of the application of the rules of 'keep promises' and 'tell the truth' to the particular situation. (I agree with Hare that this sort of weighing up is a dangerous practice. A good utilitarian would think rather differently and consider only the consequences of particular courses of action. But most people are not utilitarians, and even utilitarians are usually not good ones, as their over-riding feeling for benevolence can be contaminated by obsessions about traditional rules from which they may not be able to free themselves, even though in a cool hour they may feel these to be mere obsessions which should if necessary be over-ridden.)

Considerations about the semantics of 'ought'

How can we state the semantics for 'I have an obligation to do X and also an obligation to refrain from doing X'? Vermazen's idea of a Plan provides the solution. We can have 'Obliged $(a, t,$ "Keeps promises")' and 'Obliged $(a, t,$ "Tells the truth")', and an action which satisfies the Plan corresponding to the former sentence may not be able to satisfy the Plan corresponding to the latter sentence and *vice versa*. We may therefore hold to both 'Obliged $(a, t,$ "Keeps promises")' and 'Obliged $(a, t,$ "Tells the truth")', while denying one or other or both of 'Ought $(a, t,$ "Keeps promises")' and 'Ought $(a, t,$ "Tells the truth")', where 'Ought', unlike 'Obliged', goes with the Plan that the agent can accept all things considered. However 'all things considered' must be taken to refer to what things we are willing to consider in the circumstances. In the case of the moral 'ought', all things whatever should be considered, but in the case of other practical 'ought' sentences, the things to be considered will be those which are relevant from a particular point of view, e.g. a burglar's point of view.

THE AFFECTIVE 'OUGHT'

Suppose that we say that a man ought to feel sad in consequence of his sister's illness. This is not the practical 'ought', because feeling sad is a state of mind, not an action. Nor is the 'ought' the ought of subjective betterness; it does not correspond to a sentential operator on pain of paradoxes like that of the Good Samaritan. (If it ought to be the case that a man should feel sad in consequence of his sister's illness it would seem to follow that it ought to be the case that the sister be ill.) The sentence 'Bill ought to feel sad at Jane's illness' could be treated as 'Ought (Bill, t, "Feels sad at Jane's illness")'. Here t will refer not to an instant of time, or a fairly narrow time span centred on t, as in the practical 'ought', but to a more extensive time span over which we would like the predicate 'Feels sad' to be true of time slices of Bill. Those philosophers who for some reason that is unclear to me object to applying predicates such as 'Feels sad' to time slices or temporal stages of persons can if they like replace the '(Bill, t, "Feels sad . . .")' with '(Bill, "Feels sad at t . . .")'.

V

GOODNESS

SEMANTIC QUESTIONS

There are words such as 'right' and 'duty' that are so clearly related to 'ought' that it is unnecessary for me to discuss their semantics separately. However another favourite in the stock in trade of moral philosophers is 'good' and related words such as 'bad', 'better', 'worse'. These do need separate treatment. It is true that people often talk of an action as being 'good' in circumstances in which I would want to say that it is 'right' or 'what ought to be done'. I would recommend that this use of 'good' be avoided. The word 'right' is available to do this job. A more appropriate use of 'good action' occurs when we wish not to commend the action as such (in the abstract, or because of its consequences or its conformity with rules) but because we wish to commend the motive from which it sprang. Since one can do a right action from a bad motive and a wrong action from a good motive, it would be wise to avoid ambiguity by using 'good' and 'bad' for the motives of actions and 'right' and 'wrong' for the actions as such, without reference to their motives.

Moral philosophers have traditionally distinguished different senses of 'good'. Thus Moore distinguished 'good as an end' from 'goods as a means', or 'intrinsically good' from 'extrinsically good'. Others have distinguished 'good' as a predicate as in 'Pleasure is good' or in 'God is good', from 'good' as a predicate modifier, as in 'Bill Sikes is a good burglar', 'Jones is a good lawyer', 'That is a good screwdriver'.

I have taken the Quinean view that one should avoid reference to senses or meanings, but as in the last chapter I shall take the view that it is legitimate to distinguish senses where there is a definite syntactic difference in question.

The word 'good' is a predicate modifier, not a predicate, in 'Bill Sikes is a good burglar', 'Jones is a good lawyer' and 'That is a good screwdriver', because they do not imply 'Bill Sikes is good and is a burglar', 'Jones is good and is a lawyer', 'That is good and is a screwdriver'.[1] Jones might be a good lawyer and yet a thoroughly bad person who beat his wife, made unfair remarks about his rivals, and so on. That is, in these cases, 'good' does not behave syntactically like 'blue'. 'That is a blue flower' implies 'That is blue and is a flower'. One might be tempted to deny the syntactic differences between 'God is good' and 'Jones is a good lawyer' by supposing that 'God is good' is short for 'God is a good person'. Similarly, 'Pleasure is good' might be taken as elliptical for 'Pleasure is a good state of mind'. However this would not show what is required, because 'God is a good person' does seem to imply 'God is good and is a person' and 'Pleasure is a good state of mind' does seem to imply 'Pleasure is good and is a state of mind'. Thus I am inclined to continue to distinguish two senses (two syntactically different uses) of 'good', in one of which it is a predicate and the other of which it is a predicate modifier. Jones might be a bad person (bad and a person) and yet a good lawyer (not both good and a lawyer). We also have 'good for', as in 'This jemmy is good for opening a ground floor window'. At first this looks as though 'good' is a predicate and 'for opening a ground floor window' the associated modifier. However I think that this would be a mistake. We could deny that the jemmy was good, even though it was good for opening windows. We could also say that it was bad to have on one's person when the police arrived. Taking 'good' and 'bad' to be predicates we would have to say that the jemmy was both good and bad at the same time. I think we should take 'good for' as elliptical for 'good instrument for'. So 'good' is the modifier and 'is an instrument for . . .' is the predicate it modifies. 'For opening windows' is indeed a modifier too, but it modifies 'is an instrument', not 'is good'.

Though in Chapter 2 I took the view that whether the naturalistic fallacy is a fallacy is not a clear question, I think that

Goodness

we can say that in general the use of 'good' has something to do either with commendation or approval or answering certain purposes. Thus the religious believers who say that God is good generally do so because they have a pro-attitude to God, a pro-attitude for which 'liking' is too weak a word, not because it does not truly apply but because of the importance of feelings of awe and the numinous with which it is suffused. (It is, of course, sometimes the case that religious believers may say that God is good purely on a religious or theological authority. They will do this because of a pro-attitude to the authority.) A man who says that pleasure is good does so because he likes pleasure in itself, though he may dislike certain particular sorts of pleasures because of their effects, or because of the concomitant effects of what cause them. We may not approve of carrying firearms ourselves but may nevertheless assent to the judgment that a pistol is a good weapon for a highwayman to have, in virtue here not of our own desires and purposes but of those of the highwayman. Though we do not approve, the highwayman does.

In so far as 'good' has a purely predicative sense, as in 'God is good' or 'pleasure is good', its semantics presents no difficulty: x satisfies the predicate 'good' if and only if x is good. (As I shall suggest in the next chapter this is independent of various theories about the objectivity or subjectivity of ascriptions of goodness, though an out and out subjectivist who held that 'x is good' is equivalent to 'I approve of x' would have to modify the formula to account for indexicality: he would have to say that x satisfies the predicate 'good' as uttered by person P at time t if and only if x is good relative to P and t, i.e. if and only if x is approved by P at t. I am not myself proposing such an explicit subjectivism, though I want to appreciate an insight that lies behind it.)

What about 'good' as a predicate modifier? As far as I am aware there is no fully satisfactory semantics for predicate modifiers. Of course this is not a difficulty peculiar to ethics. A big mouse need not be big and a mouse any more than a good burglar need be good and a burglar. A big mouse is a small (not big) mammal and a good burglar is (usually) a bad (not good) citizen. So if a big mouse was big and a mouse and a small mammal was small and a mammal then a big mouse would be both big and not big. Similarly a good burglar who was a bad citizen would be both good and not good. This is why we have to say that 'big' and 'good' are (like adverbs) predicate modifiers, not predicates.

There are two favoured ways to deal with the semantics of predicate modifiers. Each has its problems. The first way is to treat the surface form directly. The second, which has been favoured by Donald Davidson, is to treat the surface form as deceptive: the idea is that at a deeper level into which the surface form can be transformed, predicate modifiers will disappear.

The trouble with the first method arises from the intensionality of predicate modifiers. The class of X's can be identical to the class of Y's and yet a good X may not be a good Y. It is natural therefore to deal with predicate modifiers by means of 'possible worlds' semantics. An intension of a predicate can be identified with a function from possible worlds to sets of sequences of entities that satisfy the predicate in these worlds. Because of the obscurities of possible worlds semantics I am not too keen on this approach, even though possibilities are obviously needed in meta-ethics somewhere and somehow. In deciding on alternative courses of action we are clearly deciding between different possibilities, not all of which can be actual. We need to think of alternative futures branching off from the moment of decision and decide which one to make actual. There is only one actual future, but it is made actual in the sense that one's decision is related in a certain causal way to events in the future. I can *cause* the future even though I cannot *change* the future. (For if I decide to do A rather than B then A is the future.) Still, making a decision does involve thinking of alternative possible future worlds. I suggest that they be construed in some non-literal way, as with Richard Jeffrey's 'complete novels' or as with Quine on set theoretic surrogates.[2] (For every sentence in the language a complete novel must contain either it or its negation.) The fact that up to the time of decision the possible worlds thus envisaged all coincide with the actual one implies that the problem of specifying what it is for something in one 'world' to be the counterpart of something in another 'world' is much mitigated. In particular all temporal continuations of the agent count as counterparts of one another.

For various reasons Donald Davidson rejects possible worlds semantics. He thus wants to give a non-intensional theory of predicate modifiers. According to the Davidsonian approach one has to suppose that 'x is a good F' is a surface form which transforms into something like '*x* is better than most *F*'s' or perhaps '*x* is better than the average *F*' or perhaps again '*x* is better than a typical *F*'.³ None of these will quite do. Most potatoes are good, and so a good potato need not be better than most potatoes. Nor will it be worse than most potatoes. We would talk in this way if some potatoes were very bad indeed, but the vast majority were much better than the bad ones. An 'average' or a 'typical' potato might be some one of the vast majority of good ones, and a good potato could be worse than an average or a typical one.⁴

Of course Davidson should not be too surprised that none of these translations work, since in general he agrees with Quine in rejecting analyticity. Nevertheless he does allow for transformations from surface grammar to deep grammar, and he believes deep grammar to be that of quantification theory (first order predicate logic). Thus in the case of another sort of predicate modifier, the adverb 'cleverly', say, he would translate 'Smith passed the ball cleverly' to 'Something was passing the ball by Smith and was clever', thus explaining the inference from 'Smith passed the ball cleverly' to 'Smith passed the ball', which is now seen to be just a matter of ordinary quantification theory (first order predicate logic).

Perhaps Davidson's theory could be saved from the difficulties about 'good potato' by supposing that the transformation rules are not unique but different on different occasions. However this would be unpalatable, I think, because it would make transformation from surface to deep grammar more than the merely mechanical thing it surely should be.

I am therefore bound to conclude that probably there is at present no fully satisfactory semantic theory for 'good' as it occurs as a predicate modifier. However the difficulties both for the direct approach (reliance on the obscurities of possible worlds semantics) and for the Davidsonian approach (lack of unique transformations from surface to deep structure) are common to all predicate modifiers: they relate to 'big' no less than to 'good'. They also relate to 'very', though this word has no use otherwise than as a modifier: syntax alone prevents us transforming 'He is very kind' into 'He is very and he is kind'.

Goodness

INTRINSIC AND EXTRINSIC GOODNESS

Some things, such as happiness, are generally thought to be good in themselves; others, such as money, are even more generally held to be good as a means. I cannot help thinking that G.E. Moore was right in thinking the distinction a fundamentally important one. It is not as clear a one as I would wish. Nevertheless, in so far as our moral thinking is consequentialist (and even deontological moral thinkers often recognize a *prima facie* duty of benevolence, and so must be consequentialist to *some* extent) the distinction between intrinsic and extrinsic goodness is fundamental, and the semantic problems connected with it cannot be escaped.

Suppose that a person says that pleasant states of mind are intrinsically good. At a first approximation, he or she would prefer a universe containing pleasant states of mind to a universe otherwise similar but not containing such states of mind, supposing that there were no effects (good or bad) of these states of mind. To avoid construing this in terms of 'possible worlds', realistically construed, we could say that he or she 'prefers-true' certain sets of sentences rather than others. Moore thought that a state of mind containing sorrow at another's suffering was intrinsically good, whereas one containing delight at another's suffering was intrinsically bad. A hedonist would say the opposite, though he or she might agree that delight at another's suffering had bad effects, such as sadistic behaviour, and so was extrinsically very bad indeed, even though it was intrinsically good. The hedonist might even have a preference for sorrow at another's misfortune over delight at another's even in cases where there were no relevant effects, but this would be because it was itself the effect of some neurological state which is apt to cause sympathy and consequent good effects. That is why I said 'At a first approximation' a few sentences back.

Suppose a hedonist were to say (as he or she must) that the pleasure that a sadist got was intrinsically good, even though it was extrinsically bad. It would be extrinsically bad in that (1) it would reinforce the tendency to sadistic behaviour in the future and (2) was the concomitant effect of activity that caused pain to others. The hedonist would have an *extrinsic* preference that the sadist not feel pleasure because of (1) and (2). He or she would still hold that the sadist's pleasure was *intrinsically* good. On the other hand an 'ideal' (non-hedonistic) utilitarian, such as Moore, would disagree. How do these philosophers know that they disagree with one another in their attitudes to sadistic pleasures? Perhaps the distinction between intrinsic and extrinsic goodness has no clear meaning, as C.L. Stevenson argued.[5] To distinguish the two sorts of goodness one would need to distinguish our intrinsic preferences from our extrinsic preferences. In the case of sadistic pleasure, the hedonist would presumably have an intrinsic preference that the sadist's pleasure should exist even though he or she had a strong extrinsic preference that it should not exist. Moore would have both an intrinsic preference and an extrinsic preference that the sadist's pleasure not exist.

So far as I can see, the only way of disentangling intrinsic and extrinsic preferences is to contemplate certain possible worlds. Consider a possible world in which sadists were always deluded: they falsely believed that they were causing suffering to others but because of some strange concomitance of events they never did in fact cause this suffering (sadistic dreams are almost like this). What should we say about the pleasure the sadists got from their deluded activities? The hedonist would have a preference for such a world over an otherwise similar world in which the sadists' states of mind were not pleasurable. Moore, on the other hand, would prefer an otherwise similar world in which the deluded sadists felt sorrow, rather than pleasure.

I suggested on the previous page that such talk of possible worlds need not be taken (as it is by David Lewis[6]) realistically. In fact on a realistic theory of possible worlds they are all going to exist anyway, and so a truly universalistic ethics collapses. Why should Smith think that he ought not to kill Jones? On the realistic theory of possible worlds there is going to be a world in which Smith (or a counterpart) kills Jones (or rather a counterpart of Jones). Also there will be one in which Smith or his counterpart does not kill Jones or his counterpart. All Smith achieves by not killing Jones is that Jones is not killed in the actual world, but the actual world is just the world in which Smith is. In *any* world a speaker will call his or her world 'actual'. (Thus Lewis has argued that 'actual' is an indexical expression.) The counterpart of Smith would call *his* world the actual one. The only sort of ethics that a realistic theory of possible worlds

Goodness

would allow would be an ethics of the speaker's own world, and this would be a particularist ethics, much as an ethics that considered only the good of one's own tribe or nation would be.

As I suggested a few pages back, it is best to elucidate possible worlds talk non-realistically in terms of set theoretic surrogates or perhaps of what Richard Jeffrey has called 'complete novels'. As I noted a few pages above, a complete and consistent novel in English is a set of English sentences such that (a) it is consistent (b) every sentence or its negation occurs in the set. We could elucidate the hedonist and Moore as disagreeing in preferring true certain complete novels or classes of complete novels.

Ethics cannot avoid talk of possible worlds, even if the talk need not be realistically interpreted. In making any practical decision one is surely doing so on the basis of a preference between possible worlds even if we construe these in terms of suitable surrogates, such as complete novels or set theoretic models. We cannot be preferring one *action* or *event* to another, because if we do *A* rather than *B* only the event doing *A* exists. Doing *B* is non-existent and so cannot be a term in a relation of preferring *A* over *B*. So reference to some surrogate for possible worlds is inevitable in a semantic treatment for ethics. In the case of the deluded sadist, what is unclear about the story is not just its 'possible world' character, but its bizarre nature. The story about the deluded sadist may strike us as contrived and hard to work out in detail. One also has the sort of worry that Quine has expressed about the fuzziness of the counterpart relation and of the similarity relation between worlds. For example, consider a possible world in which someone is snub-nosed, fought in wars, lives in somewhere like Athens, is married to someone like Xanthippe, etc., but is not a philosopher. Is such a person more nearly a counterpart of Socrates, than is someone who is a philosopher, drinks hemlock, etc., but is not snub-nosed, does not live in somewhere like Athens, etc.? Are these questions determinate enough to have a clear sense? As I mentioned earlier, worries about the counterpart relation are at least greatly mitigated in the case of the sort of different possibilities that we envisage in decision making. As I also noted above, a notion of possible worlds is needed to elucidate the distinction between intrinsic and extrinsic value. Nevertheless, whether it is very clear or not, a distinction between what is intrinsically good and what is extrinsically good (of course some things can be both) is needed in utilitarian decision making, and so I am reluctant to jettison it. I should add that the recent tendency to replace talk of maximization of intrinsic value by that of maximizing satisfaction of desire or preference does not help here. We would still need to distinguish intrinsic and extrinsic preference. If we have a desire for A in itself and a desire for B merely because it causes A, we should surely not count both these satisfactions of desire in our calculations. Satisfying the intrinsic preference is what matters, and to count the satisfying of the extrinsic preference as well would be in a sense to count the same thing twice over.[7]

'Extrinsically' and 'intrinsically' can naturally be taken as modifiers of the predicate 'good'. So also 'as a means'. But perhaps that is elliptical, so that the modifier should be given explicitly as 'as a means to happiness', say. But here we run up against semantic problems to which I do not know the answer.

EVALUATION

'Good' and 'bad' and their related words are typically thought of as value words. However they are not needed for evaluation. Whether a particular utterance of a sentence is an evaluative one is a matter of its pragmatics, not its semantics. Usually to say that someone is kind, courageous and intelligent is to praise him, to evaluate him positively. But it need not. 'Kind' and 'courageous' are thought to be value words because most people like other people to be kind and courageous. There is however no unbreakable semantic connection between 'kind' or 'courageous' and 'being liked' or 'being commended'. A rough Spartan people might consistently despise kindness, and a soft easy-going tribe might have no liking for courage.

Suppose that various persons are being considered for a position in philosophy. I may say 'So-and-so is good' or 'So-and-so is a good philosopher'. Considerations such as those I canvassed in Chapter 3 now apply. I do very little to achieve my aim of getting you to agree to so-and-so's being appointed if I just say that he or she is a good philosopher. At the very most all that you gather is that he or she possesses some qualities that I admire in philosophers. Knowing me, you will guess (if you did not already know) that so-and-so is not an existentialist or a phenomenologist. You will guess that he or she writes lucidly, possesses originality, or is an inspiring teacher. Of course you may be wrong. So-and-so may even have converted me to an interest in phenomenology. He or she may write obscurely. He or she may be a pedestrian teacher. Still, you must guess that he or she has *some* out of the range of characteristics that you believe that I admire in philosophers. Of course one of the things that could be said about so-and-so is that his or her referees think him or her good. The notice we take of this will depend on whether we think that the referees are good judges of the qualities that we admire, such as philosophical originality, and whether the qualities they admire are indeed more or less the qualities we admire.

Hence in the last resort we persuade by ascribing particular qualities, such as originality and lucidity, rather than goodness or badness themselves. Similarly with morality: we may best get someone to get the attitude to another that we want him or her to get if we say things like 'So-and-so is kind', 'So-and-so is deceitful', 'So-and-so is egotistical', 'So-and-so works hard', 'So-and-so is sensitive to other people's worries and interests', 'So-and-so is friendly', 'So-and-so is ambitious' and so on. Sometimes one may say things like 'So-and-so is over-ambitious', or 'So-and-so is not kind enough', or 'So-and-so is too egotistical'. Here 'over', 'enough', or 'too' could be paraphrased by 'ought'. A man is too egotistical if he is more egotistical than he ought to be. You can assess the value of what I say only if you have some idea how egotistical I think a person ought (or ought not) to be, and you can know this only if you know something about my own likes and dislikes as they relate to egotistical behaviour and the probable consequences of such behaviour. So I could just as usefully paraphrase 'over', 'enough' and 'too' without using 'ought' and by saying, for example, 'more ambitious than I (or you) would like him to be'.

Non-naturalists, such as Moore, put 'good' and 'bad' on the 'non-natural' side, and 'kind', 'deceitful', etc. on the 'natural' side. The considerations of the previous paragraphs suggest that the purposes of evaluation can be carried out using only the latter 'factual' terms. Some philosophers have wanted to hold that terms such as 'kind' and 'deceitful' are partly factual but also partly evaluative. I think that this is a muddle. It is utterances not sentences that are evaluative. Evaluation is a matter of the pragmatics of language, not its semantics. The only sense in saying that a term like 'kind' is evaluative is that it occurs very commonly in evaluative utterances. But there are hardly any terms applicable to persons and their motives that are never used in evaluative utterances. Evaluation goes still wider of course, e.g. 'good piece of country', 'good sunset' are possible utterances, and here too 'good' is dispensable if we can indeed persuade our audience better by being more concrete and saying 'fertile piece of country', 'many-hued sunset', or whatever.

Thus when we make moral evaluations of persons' characters we can do so purely factually, by pointing to traits of character, just as we can talk of a snake being poisonous or a sheep being docile. These descriptions do not have any evaluative meaning as such, because as I suggested 'being evaluative' is a pragmatic predicate, not a semantic one. Even the poisonousness of a snake can be favourably evaluated, as when an old-fashioned oriental despot might have decided that it would be a good one to put in his snake pit.

In Chapter 2 I suggested that none of the traditional metaethical theories was wholly adequate, though there was some truth in a number of them. In saying that a trait of character is good a person might sometimes be paraphrased in an objectivist way, as saying that the trait of character tended to make him obey some conventional moral code, or that it was admired by the tribal elders, and so on. But here too 'good' and 'bad' are not needed: the purely 'factual' remarks about the relation of the trait to moral codes, tribal elders, or what not, would do just as well pragmatically.

The semantics for 'good' (in its use as a predicate) itself provides no special problem: 'courage is good' is true if and only if courage is good. 'x is good' is satisfied by y if and only if y is good. If one held an explicitly subjectivist theory of 'good' and 'ought' one would of course have to modify the semantics to allow of an indexical element. Thus on this theory 'Courage is good' would work like 'I have a pro-attitude to courageous acts', and semantically we could say that 'Courage is good' said by person P at time t is true if and only if courage is good relative to

P at t. In fact even if there were only a *partial* truth in subjectivism we could deal with 'good' and 'ought' in this manner. In so far as the truth in subjectivism were *merely* partial the 'said by P at t' would also to some extent function like an idle wheel in the semantics. An out and out subjectivist would have to concede that 'This is good' said by Smith does not contradict 'This is not good' said by Jones at the same time and in the same context, and would have to explain the appearance of contradiction here by saying that there is a conflict in attitude between Smith and Jones which gets misconstrued as a semantic contradiction. I prefer however to take the view that there is a semantic contradiction and that 'good' and 'ought' should not be relativized to a speaker. The appearance of implications about the speaker's attitudes is now what needs to be explained, and they can be explained as Gricean 'conversational implicatures'. My reason for opting for the latter course is that the indexical or explicitly subjectivist approach gets into difficulties over negation and implication. A person may correctly report that he or she approves of making true both of two complex sentences that he or she fails to see are incompatible with one another. So on the explicitly subjectivist account both incompatible sentences would have to be true, which is impossible. Similarly a hypothetical ethical sentence may be logically true, but if the protasis and apodosis are complex a person may not believe that it is logically true and so disapprove of making true the apodosis while approving of making true the protasis. Nevertheless there is at a deeper level some truth in subjectivism. It will be recalled from Chapter 4 that being fitted to the actual ends (not necessarily the believed ends) of the speaker is one of the ways in which an action can be fitting to a situation, to revert to the looser ways of speaking that I used at the beginning of that chapter, i.e. that something of the form 'Ought (a, t, F)' can be true. In the same way 'good' can sometimes be correctly applied in virtue of the actual wants or likings of the speaker. In the following chapter I shall try to bring out the underlying truth (or partial truth) in subjectivism or at least of what the subjectivist should be trying to get at, despite an objectivist looking formal semantics.

VI

ETHICS, TRUTH AND FACT

SEMANTICS AND FACTS

In Chapters 2 and 5 I have suggested that ethical statements using 'ought' and 'good' and so on are not factual, but are concerned with persuasion, analogous to imperatives, or in so far as they are factual are concerned with social facts (the wishes of the tribal elders, concordance with a conventional moral code) or perhaps the reference presupposed may be to a supposed theological fact, such as the will of God. Or again, they may be concerned with subjective facts about the attitudes or desires of the speaker.

Nevertheless I have denied that on any occasion such ethical statements can be *translated* (as opposed to paraphrased) into sociological, theological or psychological statements of fact. Nor can they be translated into imperatives, even though pragmatically imperatives would be as useful (or indeed as useless). I have also held that ethical statements involving 'ought', 'good' and so on fit the Tarski truth paradigm perfectly well.

I want to say that science, history, and so on, are concerned with finding out what the world is like, whereas in ethics we are concerned with what to do about the world. Thus in deciding whether abortion is right or wrong we are not finding out facts, but deciding what to do about the facts or what to encourage others to do about them. (Though of course biological – and some would say theological – facts are very relevant to making up our minds about what to do.)

The trouble is that this talk of facts is metaphysically suspect.

Ethics, truth and fact

Wittgenstein in the *Tractatus*[1] said that the world consists of facts, not of things. I want to say (more in accordance with common sense) that the world consists of things not of facts[2] – physical particles, perhaps space-time points, possibly even abstract entities such as numbers and sets of them. But not facts.

Wittgenstein's theory in the *Tractatus* was a picture theory, a correspondence theory of truth. Sentences pictured facts. As I have learned from Donald Davidson, the picture theory goes with substitutional quantification, whereas Tarski's account of truth goes with the notion of satisfaction of predicates. In the former theory sentences relate to facts whereas in the latter objects, or sequences of them, relate to predicates.

Indeed in the *Tractatus* Wittgenstein's account of quantification is implicitly substitutional. He elucidates '$(x)Fx$' as '$Fa, Fb, Fc \ldots$' where 'a', 'b', etc. are all the names of all the objects. Since such an expression could not be written down (especially if there are infinitely many objects in the world) we should suppose that what Wittgenstein is saying is that '$(x)Fx$' is true if and only if 'Fx' becomes a true sentence if we substitute any name whatever for the 'x'. This theory of quantification has been cogently criticized by Quine.[3] We just do not have names for all objects. Nor *could* we have such if there are non-denumerably many objects in the world. Looking at the matter from the point of view of objectual quantification we can see that the set of real numbers for example is non-denumerable, even though the advocate of substitutional quantification would not be able to accept Cantor's proof that there are non-denumerable sets. So, as Quine acknowledges, the argument from non-denumerability will not work against the defender of substitutional quantification, since Cantor's argument assumes objectual quantification. Nevertheless, as Quine contends, we do not need this argument. The argument against substitutional quantification can rest on the fact that we can use sentences containing 'all kangaroos' or 'some wombats' even though we have not got a name for each kangaroo or wombat.

Davidson's theory of truth is a Tarski-type one. Instead of the relation of sentences to facts, as in the picture theory, there is the relation of satisfaction which an object or sequence of objects bears to a predicate.[4] The theory gives a relation between language and the world and so is in the *spirit* of the correspondence theory of truth. (As against, say, the traditional coherence theory, which can be more sensibly interpreted as a theory of warranted assertibility. Warranted assertibility differs from truth, since a warrantedly assertible sentence may by bad luck be false, and a true sentence may not be warrantedly assertible, since we may have no good evidence for it.)

In any case there is something difficult about the notion of a fact. Davidson has argued that if true sentences correspond to facts then there can be only one fact.[5] He makes the plausible assumption that logically equivalent true sentences correspond to the same fact. In that case the fact that p is the same fact as the fact that $(\imath x)(x=t \cdot p) = (\imath x)(x=t)$, since this last sentence is logically equivalent to p. (Here t is some object.) But if q is true it corresponds to the same fact as $(\imath x)(x=t \cdot q)$ and $(\imath x)(x=t \cdot p) = (\imath x)(x=t \cdot q)$. So if $\ulcorner p \urcorner$ and $\ulcorner q \urcorner$ are both true they correspond to the same fact. There can be only one fact.

This argument is evaded by Barry Taylor[6] who allows only *tightly* logically equivalent sentences to express the same facts. A logical equivalence is said by him to be 'tight' if and only if it is derivable from first order logic without the axioms relating to identity or to the description operator. However Taylor's own account of facts (or 'situations') depends on a theory of possible worlds. That this is necessary can be seen from the consideration that in the actual world true sentences using different but co-extensive predicates are commonly supposed to correspond to different facts. Thus it would seem to be the case that 'Quine is a terrestrial creature with a kidney' and 'Quine is a terrestrial creature with a backbone' correspond to different facts, even though 'terrestrial creature with kidney' and 'terrestrial creature with backbone' are co-extensive predicates. So we need to consider possible worlds other than the actual world in which these predicates are not co-extensive. Taylor therefore has to modify the ordinary Tarski-type semantics to a Kripke-type one, in which the idea is not satisfaction *simpliciter* but satisfaction in world w. There are Davidsonian objections to this (truth is no longer disquotational). I have conceded that some notion of possible worlds is needed in ethics and practical decision theory generally (though they may be surrogate or ersatz ones). One would prefer not to have it in metaphysics, however, and a general theory of facts is metaphysics and not ethics.

Nevertheless even if we allow Taylor's semantic elucidation of

Ethics, truth and fact

'state of affairs' (or 'fact' in the case of true sentences) we still have difficulty in saying clearly that ethics is not factual. Let us suppose that in some Taylorian sense true sentences do correspond to facts. This does not help with the concern of the present chapter, which is to defend the notion that in some sense science, history, etc. state facts about the world, whereas (with the qualifications already made) ethics is not factual. Since ethics is expressible with indicative sentences, and 'ought' is a predicate, not an intensional operator (see Chapter 4), true 'ought' sentences would correspond to Taylorian facts no less than scientific ones about hydrogen and oxygen, and so on. It is not easy to deny that 'ought' sentences can be true: 'Smith ought to be kind to his grandmother' is true if and only if Smith ought to be kind to his grandmother, no less than 'snow is white' is true if and only if snow is white. So even if we accept Taylor's semantics of states of affairs, this does not help those of us who want to say that science is about the facts of the world, whereas ethics is not about facts (with the qualifications already made) but is about what to do about the facts of the world.

I think that we have to hold, therefore, that the question of whether ethics is factual is not a matter that can be decided by technical semantics. I think that it has to be decided by the most plausible theory, in the light of total science, including sociology, of how ethical language functions in our lives. Of course, as I argued in Chapters 3 and 5, specifically ethical language is not needed for persuasion anyway. The use of 'ought' and 'good' and their cognates are related to desire while scientific language is related to belief. (Except in so far as 'ought' and 'good' relate to sociological or psychological fact.) The imperativist theory of ethics tries to capture this theory of ethics semantically, but the applicability of the Tarski paradigm to ethical indicative sentences frustrates this approach. Remember that on page 17 I remarked that the introduction of quantifiers makes a theory of compliance conditions parasitic on one of truth conditions.

BELIEFS AND MAPS

I have just argued that even Taylor's introduction of facts would not help in my attempt to characterize ethical language, since semantically ethical sentences would fall on the side of 'fact'. I suggest that we give up 'fact' for 'factual', and this leads us beyond semantics. (Some sentences with a Tarski semantics of truth or satisfaction conditions will be 'factual' and some will not be so.) Nor (for reasons that I have given) do I want to accept a picture theory of language. Nevertheless I think that it is helpful to consider a picture theory of *belief*. I do not want to say that all beliefs are very like pictures. For example, how would a belief of the form $(\exists x)Fx$ or its negation be a picture? Can you picture quarks? And so on. Nevertheless I think that it is legitimate and useful to *compare* beliefs (not sentences!) with pictures, or more particularly with maps. I make this comparison in order to try to make clearer the bearing of my contention that in science, history, etc., we are trying to find out what the world is *like*, whereas in ethics we are trying to decide what to *do*. (Here doing includes encouraging or discouraging others to do.) When one tries to come to an answer about some difficult moral problem, for example concerned with the rights and wrongs of abortion, one is not trying to discover some elusive fact about the world but trying to decide what to do, for example whether to support or oppose the practice of abortion. And yet I have to recognize the fact that it is good colloquial English for someone to say 'I believe that abortion is right' or 'I believe that abortion is wrong'. Some people may even say 'I *know*' or 'It is a *fact* that abortion is wrong'. So on the theory I am advocating we would have to say that colloquial English should sometimes be taken as misleading at least. I can of course fully agree that matters of fact are *relevant* to deciding whether abortion is right or wrong. Factual beliefs can canalize our ultimate desires (and also our non-ultimate desires) in the manner discussed in Chapter 3. (This goes back to Hume.) But our *ultimate* desires are not themselves determined by factual beliefs.

I need to be able to say, therefore, that someone's so-called 'belief' that abortion is wrong, say, is not really a belief. It may really be a desire – a desire to oppose abortion. And a so-called 'belief' that abortion is right may be a desire to support or engage in abortion. I need a theory of belief that does not rest on what we colloquially call 'belief'. I want to say that so-called differences of 'ethical belief' are better described as differences of ultimate attitude or desire. Or rather I would want to say this in

Ethics, truth and fact

many contexts. It may be that sometimes ethical 'ought' statements may be paraphrased in purely cognitive terms. For example in paraphrasing an 'ought' statement uttered by someone like Jeanie Deans we might refer to alleged facts about God's commandments as reported in the Bible. But even such a person's statements count as ethical because of this person's *desire*, whether from love of God or fear of hell, to obey these supposed commandments.

I wish therefore not to produce an *analysis* of belief, but to make some *comparisons*. Following F.P. Ramsey[7] and D.M. Armstrong[8] let us compare beliefs with maps. Ramsey said that 'A belief of the primary sort is a map . . . by which we steer'. I shall ignore Ramsey's distinction indicated by the words 'of the primary sort'. Ramsey is concerned with the relation of belief to practice, and the 'by which we steer' distinguishes the believing of a proposition from the mere entertaining of a proposition. Nevertheless many factual beliefs are of little or no consequence in practical decision making. Consider for example a belief about quarks or about undiscovered writings by Horace. Even so there are theoretical decisions to be made, namely as whether or not to assert the corresponding propositions, whether or not to incorporate them in our web of belief, whether it is worthwhile to write a paper on quarks or a book on Horace, and so on. The difference is like that between a map of Tibet, even though we never intend to go there or have any political or business or cultural dealing with Tibetans, and a map of the fictional pirate island in R.L. Stevenson's *Treasure Island*. Nevertheless in discussing ethics we are in the nature of the case particularly concerned with beliefs that are practically relevant, even though they may in a sense be highly theoretical, as is the case with beliefs about the fission of uranium 235 or the fusion of hydrogen.

We can talk of believing-true a sentence S. This is so even with many indexical sentences. If Jones believes that he *is* Jones (has not lost his memory) we can suppose that if he says 'I am tall' that he believes-true 'Jones is tall'. However as John Perry[9] has shown there are essentially indexical beliefs. Suppose that I believe at 12.00 noon that a bomb will explode in ten minutes' time, but do not know the time. I do not believe-true that a bomb will explode at noon plus ten minutes. What I do is to

Ethics, truth and fact

believe-true of now (or to state the theory more generally of me-now) the predicate or open sentence 'there is a bomb explosion ten minutes later than . . .'. Similar treatment is needed for sentences like 'You are here' on a library diagram, which can be helpful even though you are unable beforehand to distinguish where you are by any uniquely referring predicate. I think that this 'essential indexical' may perhaps need to be considered for some problems in decision theory and hence ethics, but I propose to put it aside at present, since to make the distinctions that are relevant in this chapter it will do to consider only cases in which it is safe to talk of believing-true a sentence. More complications should not be imported into a discussion than are needed for the problem at hand.

A map differs from a sentence or set of sentences because of its non-discrete character. In many maps indefinitely many propositions can be read off by a map reader who reads off distances and directions between points, heights above sea level, and so on. This may be limited only by the finite grain of the photographs from which the map is made, and so on. Nevertheless it is clear that one can extract information from a map that is expressible in the discrete sentences of a language.

A map is a sort of picture. It is indeed a picture in the extended and abstract use of this word that we find in Wittgenstein's *Tractatus*. And so, of course, according to Wittgenstein in the *Tractatus* are many other things, such as (atomic) sentences and the wavy grooves on a gramophone record. Now I do not want to press this analogy too far and certainly it is not possible literally to picture facts about quarks, for example. Nor, as I suggested on pages 94-7, should we want facts in our ontology. What I do want is not facts but the notion of 'factual', whereby a belief does not qualify as being factual merely because we can apply the Tarski paradigm '$\ulcorner p \urcorner$ is true if and only if p' to a sentence that expresses it (a sentence that is 'believed-true'). This would let in too much. The analogy of a belief with a map does help a little bit, but not perhaps as much as I would wish.

A map is in itself desire-neutral, even though one may of course conjecture a person's desires from the maps he or she prefers to use. If he uses mainly 1:25,000 maps with contour lines every ten metres of altitude he or she is probably a bush walker or hill walker, whereas if he or she uses mainly road maps he or she is probably a traveller in motor cars. In spite of this the map in itself is desire-neutral. Consider a 1:25,000 map showing a swamp in a valley between steep hills. This does not specify any route. The representation of the swamp may indicate the locus of part of a preferred route between two hills, desired by a person who does not mind getting his or her feet wet or who likes looking for swamp dwelling birds. Equally it may indicate a route to be avoided by someone who wants to keep his or her feet dry or who fears swamp dwelling snakes. The map itself does not specify any routes. We need desires as well. In fact if beliefs are like maps this consideration supports the thesis that actions are caused jointly by beliefs and desires. A map induces certain beliefs. These beliefs may themselves, as Ramsey suggested, be importantly like maps. Of course a map can also induce a desire, but this is analogous to the way in which a belief can canalize a desire, in the manner suggested in Chapter 3. The map induces a desire by causing a belief that canalizes a desire. A map can induce a desire to cross a swamp, but this is only because it induces a belief that canalizes a more general desire, for example to take the shortest route or to see water birds.

In the *Tractatus* Wittgenstein says (6.41) 'In the world everything is as it is, and everything happens as it does happen: *in* it no value exists – and if it did exist, it [i.e. the value] would have no value'.[10] I connect this with the desire-neutrality of a map: how we want to act on the information about the swamp depends on our more general desires, such as whether to take the shortest route or to see water birds, and whether we mind getting our legs wet.

The naturalist could reply that an act of kindness or of malice, for example, could be perfectly well pictured, at least in a motion picture. And I suggested on page 33 that there is *some* truth in naturalism. Nevertheless I suggested also on page 37 that people could differ about the value of kindness (though not, I hope, the sort of people with whom I have to deal!). Therefore it seems better to say that it is kindness, not the value of kindness, that is pictured in the motion picture. But the matter is not cut and dried. As I suggested in Chapter 2, in a closed tribal society what ought to be done could be presented very much as a question of what is enjoined by the tribal elders, and this could be presented

Ethics, truth and fact

in a motion picture. Similarly Jeanie Deans (see page 12) could well be thought of as considering moral questions very largely as factual questions about what is written in the Bible and questions about what will happen to her in the last judgment if she performs certain acts.

Still, as we become more liberated and reflective persons, subjectivist theories of ethics, even though they do not provide a correct semantic analysis of ethical language, do come much nearer to showing us what the point of ethical language is. Thus a liberated and reflective person will come to judge his or her ethical principles on the basis of his or her desires – not just any desire but his or her over-riding desires (or attitudes). Thus he or she will come to assert 'X is right' or 'Y is good' if he or she has an over-riding pro-attitude to doing X or to the existence of Y.[11] Our over-riding attitude, it must be remembered (see page 10) is not necessarily our strongest attitude, but it is the one that is strongest in times of quiet reflection and is an attitude which consists in part of a disposition to do things which will strengthen or weaken certain of our lower order desires.

This consideration throws light on Mackie's 'projection theory' that I discussed in Chapter 3, and which goes back to David Hume. Even though a positive desire for X to be done or Y to exist may, on the subjectivist view, justify us in saying 'X is right' or 'Y is good' we cannot translate a sentence of the form 'X is good' as 'I have a pro-attitude to X'. This is at least partly because of its occurrence in hypothetical sentences, and because of other logical connections between sentences of the same general form. We may not be aware, for example, that two such sentences are incompatible. So we may have pro-attitudes to two inconsistent propositions being true. For reasons of this sort (see page 41) there is a tendency to speak as if objectively even when the basis of our evaluation is a matter of our desires. This tendency is strengthened by the fact that in less liberated circles ethical discourse may partake of the factual, and be decided by considerations such as the decrees of tribal elders or of the writings found in the Bible. Thus we may talk as though Mackie's projection theory were correct, but without the metaphysics of non-natural qualities that Mackie associates with it.[12]

Ethics, truth and fact
PRACTICAL CONSEQUENCES

The view of ethics as based on desire is not technically a semantic theory, but as was suggested on page 97 it is based on general considerations of scientific plausibility about the place of ethical discourse in our lives. It has some affinities to objective forms of naturalism and some to subjectivism. The fact-value dichotomy is replaced by the belief-desire dichotomy. The theory has some affinities to Mackie's projection theory.

Some readers will be put off by such a point of view. Objectivist theories of ethics are felt to be attractive because it is felt that subjectivist theories strike at the very foundations of morality. It may be thought that if we recognize that ethics depends on our desires, rather than on dispassionate reason or perception of the non-natural, we will lose motivation to behave ethically. This is a popular view, but if we look at it from a certain angle it appears quite paradoxical. If ethics depends on desires, and we have these desires, then we have all the ethical motivation we could want there to be. Indeed it is non-naturalist theories that make it difficult to relate ethics to motivation. Still, psychological mechanisms are odd, and I well remember from my undergraduate days, when I believed G.E. Moore's non-naturalism, the almost religious feeling that ethical thought produced in me, how the idea of maximizing the amount of non-natural goodness in the world came to seem enveloped in a sort of numinous golden cloud. So perhaps confusion of thought can help motivation. We must not, however, rush to the opposite extreme, and forget how motivating can be perfectly ordinary desires, for example that of generalized benevolence, the desire for the happiness of all sentient beings, which is the basis of utilitarian ethics. Again the desire to respect personal autonomy can be the basis for another sort of ethics. Given any system of ethics, we can look for the perfectly natural desires that motivate it.

It is sometimes thought that subjectivism leads to relativism. That is not true. To have a desire expressed by ethical principle *P* is not to have a wishy-washy tolerance for persons who have ethical principles opposed to *P*. Our desires will conflict. Of course in some cases tolerance may be the best course – for example a utilitarian may often be wise to tolerate those with other ethical principles, because of the consequential value of toleration and of cool persuasion as opposed to hot confrontation. But such toleration is by no means built in to the meta-ethical view that I am advocating, even though it is allowed by it.

That subjectivism does not lead to lack of moral desire is borne out well by the empirical facts. There is abundant testimony to the outstanding virtuousness of David Hume's character. 'Even in the lowest state of his fortune,' wrote Adam Smith, 'his great and necessary frugality never hindered him from exercising, upon proper occasions, acts both of charity and generosity.' This is only one of many reports of Hume's virtue in Adam Smith's letter to Strahan, which was published in 1777 along with Hume's *My Own Life*, which Hume wrote only a few weeks before his death, and which is the modest biography (only a few pages long) of a clearly most lovable man.[13] G.L. Cawkwell, in his obituary of John Mackie in the *University College Record* (Oxford), made much of Mackie's exceptional moral rectitude and said, 'An unphilosophical man, whose principal evidence about other people's conduct was the behaviour of John Mackie, could never dream of explaining it in terms of "moral scepticism".' This is not surprising, perhaps. If ethics is a matter of desire, then if people have the sort of desires (benevolence, love of justice, or whatever) that we like then they will tend to do what we like. The question of moral scepticism or of subjectivism is in this respect practically irrelevant.

OTHER DESIRES

On page 102 I suggested that ethical principles are judged on the basis of over-riding, or higher order, desires. This comes near to the sort of essentialism about ethics that I have wanted to avoid. However I do not regard this suggestion as an analytic or exceptionless truth. After all, people are often in the mood to be driven by lower order desires, which can be stronger than the higher order desires. We have the well-known phenomenon of weakness of will. Now in much of the sort of discourse that is properly called 'ethical' we sometimes appeal to at least *other* people's lower order desires. This of course chimes in well with the sort of account that I have been trying to give of ethical discourse and ethical persuasion.

Ethics, truth and fact

Sometimes the matter is still more subtle, and rhetoric may be concerned with damping down or taking care not to provoke certain transitory lower order desires. Let us return to Jeanie Deans in *The Heart of Midlothian*. In the story, after Jeanie's journey to London, largely on foot, she obtains, through the good offices of the Duke of Argyle, an interview with Queen Caroline. The Duke puts the case to the Queen, but the Queen cannot resist an argument, and makes some defence of the draconian law under which Jeanie's sister's life is forfeit. We may suppose that the Queen's undoubted benevolence and sympathy is such that on quiet reflection she would regret her argumentative sally on the other side. So after the Queen put forward her argument,

> The Duke saw and avoided the snare, for he was conscious that, by replying to the argument, he must have been inevitably led to a discussion, in the course of which the Queen was likely to be hardened in her own opinion, until she became obliged, out of mere respect to consistency, to let the criminal suffer. (Sir Walter Scott, *The Heart of Midlothian*, Chapter 36)

The Queen's respect for consistency here was presumably not of the sort that a philosopher or scientist ought to have, but is more like a desire to adhere to previous resolutions, a sort of obstinacy. The Duke therefore broke off the argument and requested the Queen to listen to Jeanie. Here we are already within a region in which ethical discourse merges into rhetoric.

VII

'OUGHT', 'CAN', FREE WILL AND RESPONSIBILITY

'OUGHT' AND 'CAN'

Moral philosophers have frequently asserted that 'ought' implies 'can'. Certainly there is little point in my saying to Jim that he ought to write a letter to his mother if Jim is illiterate. This consideration, however, is not decisive. There may be other cases in which there is point in saying 'ought' while denying 'can'. Even if there are not, we still need to ask whether it is part of the semantics of 'ought' or only of pragmatics. It is indeed hard to see how it could be part of the semantics, at least if we reject analyticity. 'If Jim ought to write to his mother he can write to his mother' does not seem to exemplify a valid schema of formal logic. Perhaps it could be said that 'No one ought to do what he cannot do' is (though not analytic) a very well-entrenched sentence of our belief system (or system of desires). Even this is doubtful. I have taken the view in previous chapters that 'ought' and 'good' are very context-dependent. So it would have to be the sentence in a context that is said to be well entrenched, when we say that 'No one ought to do what he cannot do' is well-entrenched. Certainly in some contexts it seems natural to say things like 'Of course he ought to have rescued her from drowning, but unfortunately he could not swim'.

According to Vermazen's semantics, which I advocated in Chapter 4, 'ought' is a triadic predicate of an agent, a time, and a predicate, and its semantics is elucidated by reference to a sequence of an agent, a time and a Plan.

It will be recalled that Vermazen's notion of a Plan involved that of physical necessity. Thus in the omelette example, we have it that 'is a using of butter' is not one of the predicates in the Plan, since the agent could use margarine. 'Is a breaking of eggs' would be a predicate in the Plan since it is (we may suppose) physically necessary to break eggs if one is to make an omelette. So at first sight it would appear that 'ought' does semantically imply 'can', since actions physically impossible to the agent are ruled out. (We may take 'physically impossible' to cover also 'psychologically impossible'. For physicalists the latter will include the former anyway.) However Vermazen reasonably takes the view that there is no reason why a Plan should not include a sequence of predicates of action, such that the sequence of action types so specified may include action types that the agent is unable to perform.[1] That is, the physical necessity involved in the Plan could be a relation of external physical necessity between action types: the question of whether the action types themselves are possible is another matter.

That is, it is physically necessary that an omelette maker breaks eggs, whether or not it is physically possible for a particular omelette maker to break an egg in the first place. It is physically possible to make an omelette using butter whether or not it is physically possible for a particular agent to use butter.

The conception of physical necessity that I have in mind here is that of model-theoretic consistency with the laws of nature, given a certain range of variation of the initial conditions. I shall have more to say on this topic when I discuss determinism. Now suppose that it is physically impossible for Jim to break an egg. When we say that it is physically necessary that Jim break an egg if he is to make an omelette we must consider some possible circumstances in which an agent in Jim's position, but who is able to break an egg, wishes to make an omelette. To say that it is physically necessary to break an egg to make an omelette is to say that all models of the laws of nature, together with possible initial conditions, which contain the making of an omelette or its appropriate model-theoretic surrogate also contain a breaking of an egg, or its model-theoretic surrogate.

As I noted on page 89, this may be felt to be very unclear.

Even if the models are not taken as literally real possible worlds, as envisaged by David Lewis, the notion of Jim's counterpart in the model, a surrogate for a person very like Jim but who is able to break eggs, is an imprecise one. This imprecision seems to be unavoidable. Indeed this imprecision is an unavoidable feature of ethical discourse anyway, quite independent of ' "ought" implies "can" '. When I am thinking of various alternatives of action I consider various alternatives each of which we would do if we decided or chose to do so. Suppose that in fact I decide to do A. If determinism is true, all models of the universe that contain the initial conditions (or their surrogates) and that satisfy the laws of nature (or their surrogates) are models that contain A or its surrogate. So even in any considered practical decision, ethical, burglarious, or whatever, the language in which that decision is thought out requires a possible worlds semantics. Thus if possible worlds semantics is far from precise or clear, this much imprecision or obscurity is an inescapable feature of ethics and of practice generally. The situation is hardly worse with the matter, considered in the previous three paragraphs, of a Plan (in Vermazen's sense) as applied to someone who cannot act in accordance with it. To this extent, then, I think we can say that 'ought' does not imply 'can'.

We may agree, however, that it is usually pointless to say to someone that he ought to do something when it is the case that he cannot do it. This is so when a person is physically unable to do the action, or is unable to do it because of ignorance of how to do it. But it is so also when a person is merely unmotivated to do it (recall Chapter 3). Vermazen considers a missionary who says 'that the contented heathen ought to accept Christ'.[2] Vermazen remarks that the missionary's words do not constitute a misuse or pointless use of language and the missionary need not be pretending to himself that the heathens' motivations could be made other than they are. Any infelicity in the missionary's language is not a semantic one but a pragmatic one.

DETERMINISM

Of course there will be those who will say that if the universe is deterministic (as it is not, but as will be explained shortly, any indeterminism in it is irrelevant to ethics) then we can do only what we actually do. In which case if 'ought' implied 'can' we could never say that a person ought to do something other than what he or she in fact does. The considerations of the previous section suggest the answer to this move, but I now want to go a little deeper into the matter, and discuss the freedom of the will in relation to determinism and indeterminism.

The line I wish to take is that if we can extract a common-sense concept of free will from the welter of rather confused talk on the subject that we find in ordinary life, newspaper editorials about punishment, sermons on the problem of evil, and so on and so forth, we really have to take the view that this concept is inconsistent, or as near to inconsistent as an informal concept can be. That is, it can be saved from inconsistency only by philosophically implausible suppositions. To put it crudely, the plain man expects a free action to be determined (by the agent's character) so that it is not a matter of pure chance, but nevertheless he wants it to be undetermined too. If this common-sense notion of freedom is to be saved we need to find a concept of being undetermined which is not a matter of pure chance and which makes a free action depend on the agent without being caused by the character of the agent. I think that this is, to say the least, a very dubious enterprise.

To make the discussion more precise I need to explain the notion of determinism. The most famous definition of determinism was that given by the Marquis P.S. de Laplace, near the beginning of his *Philosophical Essay on Probabilities*.[3] Laplace imagines a superior intelligence such that, if it were given the laws of nature together with the state of the universe at any one time t_o, it could calculate the state of the universe at any earlier or later time. To say that determinism is true is to say that the world is correctly described by a deterministic theory. Laplace's definition comes near to saying that the state of the universe at any time t as described within the language of classical mechanics is deducible from the state at t_o of the universe (as so described) where $t \neq t_o$. (The last clause could indeed be omitted because the case of $t = t_o$ is trivial.) If we imagine the theory of classical mechanics completely formalized then the talk of a supreme calculator could be regarded as a mere metaphor, to be replaced by the theory of formal deducibility, which is part of syntax and expressible in elementary number theory, provided that the state of the universe at t_o could be described in finitely many symbols. In classical mechanics as modified by special relativity this condition could in a sense be met, since in predicting what happens at a certain point at time t it would be necessary to consider only those particles within a radius $|c(t-t_o)|$ of that point. However there is a further problem, which is that no analytic solution to the n-body problem in classical mechanics is known. (Laplace himself was of course well aware of the difficulties posed by the n-body problem; he was indeed the great pioneer in this branch of applied mathematics.) I gather that it has not been proved that no such solution exists, even though it seems *likely* that there is no such solution. If indeed there is no such solution at all, not even knowable to God, then the supreme calculator envisaged by Laplace could not have deduced the state of the universe at t. The supreme calculator would have to proceed by approximative methods. It is not clear that these could be specified purely syntactically.

Other problems for the Laplacean sort of definition arise from various other considerations of varying importance. (1) Is the supreme calculator using a language based on a finite number of primitive symbols? If so, there are only denumerably many sentences of the language. So the calculator could not predict the state of the universe at every space-time point.[4] This is not too important an objection, I think. With reasonable assumptions of continuity it would presumably be enough if the calculator could predict the state at every rational point. (2) Given premisses at least as strong as elementary number theory, as would be the case in a scientific theory, not all model theoretic consequences of the axioms will be deducible. (This is a corollary of Gödel's theorem.) It is not clear how serious an obstacle this would be to the supreme calculator, but the problem will be taken care of when we give up a basically syntactic account of determinism for a semantic one. (3) Would the supreme calculator have to interact with the world in order to ascertain initial conditions? If so, even a deterministic calculator which was an interacting part of a deterministic world might be unable to predict (even approximately). Thus, as Sir Karl Popper has argued,[5] a classical predictor mechanism strongly interacting with another such could not predict the other's behaviour. Roughly A would have to take into account the state of B but the state of B would affect the state of A. So A would have to know its own state, but the knowing of its own state would alter that state to something else. It would thus have to take into account its taking into account of its taking into account . . . *ad infinitum*.[6] So perhaps Laplace's supreme intelligence would have to be God, who could know the state of the world without interacting with it. Obviously a lot still remains obscure here.

Thus a model-theoretic account of determinism seems preferable to Laplace's definition in terms of deducibility. Model-theoretic definitions of determinism have been rather thoroughly investigated by Richard Montague.[7] Classical mechanics provides the paradigm of a deterministic theory, quantum mechanics of an indeterministic one. We should look with suspicion on any definition of determinism that made classical mechanics anything other than deterministic.

Consider a momentary state S_o of the universe in classical particle mechanics. This state is a function from individual particles to ordered pairs of positions and velocities. Assuming that S_o can be specified, add this specification of S_o to the axioms of classical particle mechanics, including those that give the relevant laws of force. Then the system is deterministic in the sense that there is only one standard model of S_o together with the axioms. Thus there is only one possible state of the universe at any other time S_t. Putting it vividly in terms of 'possible universes', we can say that there is only one possible universe containing S_o and consistent with the laws of nature. However the tendentious talk of possible worlds can be avoided by talking of certain models definable in set theory. The general idea can be illustrated by the simple case of a universe containing exactly n classical particles. The positions and velocities of these particles can be represented by the position of a particle in a $6n$ dimensional space (for each particle three dimensions for each of position and velocity). Let us also simplify the example by supposing that no particles collide with one another, so that there are no instantaneous changes of velocity. The system is deterministic in the sense that the representative particle traces out a single line in the $6n$ dimensional space: only one such line through any given point is consistent with the laws of mechanics.[8]

The model-theoretic approach enables us to avoid worries

about the n-body problem in classical mechanics, to which I have already alluded. The marvellous precision of the approximative methods that are used in celestial mechanics is facilitated by the fact that the masses of the planets are small compared with that of the sun, and by the fact that (as Laplace was the first to prove) the solar system is stable. In other cases the situation is not so good. Astronomers can certainly investigate the future behaviour of a star cluster, to investigate its relative stability and whether it will develop into perhaps a globular or a spiral form. (In stellar dynamics the galaxy is thought of as smoothed out into a homogeneous body which acts unitarily on stars under investigation, so that a star is thought of as acted on only by nearby stars together with this homogeneous mass.) To make absolutely precise predictions far into the future is another matter. Whether even an infinite calculator could do so raises interesting problems. One might wonder whether, for suitable n and t, to calculate approximately the state at t might require more symbols than there are particles in the universe. Would this matter for Laplace's definition? The model-theoretic definition sidesteps these problems.

It should be noted that the notion of a deterministic theory is holistic. We talk about one whole state of the universe (or in relativistic mechanics of a sizeable part of the universe) determining a further state of the universe or of part of the universe. Determinism is not defined by means of the common-sense terminology of cause and effect. Nevertheless a certain restrained use of the notion of a causal chain can be elucidated in an approximate way in terms of the notion of a deterministic system. This will do something to link the physicist's concept of causality to the common-sense one.

CAUSAL CHAINS

Sometimes a system is relatively isolated from its surroundings and may develop in a relatively linear way which epitomizes something like the pattern of what common sense thinks of as a causal chain. An example of such a system would be a nerve impulse moving along an axon. The system 'axon with nerve impulse moving along it' can be regarded for many purposes as an isolated one: it can be regarded as deterministic to a high approximation so that there is no pressing need to regard it as part of a wider and more isolated system. For these purposes it has to be assumed that the surroundings remain relatively stable: for example my nervous system would not function in the normal way if all the air were suddenly removed from the room in which I am now sitting. Let us call a relatively isolated system of this sort 'a basic causal chain'. Then think of a tree in which basic causal chains come together at nodes, just as the branches of an ordinary tree do. A path through the tree, from top to bottom, will trace out a non-basic causal chain. Thus a causal chain in general need not be *always* relatively isolated from its surroundings. The notion of causality is less well understood than that of determinism.[9] However, I shall make use of the notion of causality to the extent that for present purposes we can think of it in terms of approximately deterministic and partially isolated systems.

A DILEMMA

Having got out of the way these preliminaries about the definition of determinism and the concept of causality, I wish to discuss the following dilemma.

(1) If determinism is true than our actions are determined by some previous state of the universe. Determinism implies that if the state of the universe at some time t_o is S_o, then consistently with this and with the laws of nature at any other time t there is only one state S_t of the universe. So we do not have free will.

(2) If determinism is not true then our actions may happen by pure chance. How could we be said to act freely if our action did not flow from our character, our beliefs and desires, and hence be determined by a state of the universe that included our neurophysiological 'programming'? If an action happened by pure chance, might we not find ourselves, to our horror, doing something we did not want to do, such as eating a toad? Would not such indeterminism take away our freedom?

(3) Conclusion: whether the universe is deterministic or indeterministic we do not have free will.

Of course if we believe modern physics (as we should) we must believe that the universe is indeterministic. Nevertheless it approximates to determinism at the macroscopic level. (Neurons, and even protein molecules, are macroscopic by quantum mechanical standards.) It is therefore likely that the nervous system should be considered as a deterministic mechanism. It is perhaps not absolutely impossible that it might contain an unstable mechanism that might detect certain indeterministic effects, as has been suggested by Sir John Eccles, but I shall put this possibility to one side for the moment. Then we must say that if we do have free will this must be because sub-argument (1) is unsound. And very many philosophers have indeed held that it is unsound. Indeed R.E. Hobart, in a most influential article, has argued that determinism is necessary for free will, or at least that an approximation to determinism is. The worse the approximation the less we are free.[10]

DISCUSSION OF SUB-ARGUMENT (1)

I am inclined to think that the plain man's concept of free will is inconsistent: it has evolved from a suspect theological and metaphysical climate of opinion. Nevertheless determinism allows us to go a long way towards giving the plain man what he wants from his concept of free will, and it allows us to justify also many of the distinctions that morality and the criminal law make when they ascribe or do not ascribe full or partial responsibility for actions. That is, it is certainly possible for the determinist to approximate to most of the distinctions that the man in the street wants to make or are needed for the law.

The distinctions in question are concerned with two sorts of issue. One of these is whether our actions flow from our choices and our character or whether we are coerced or compelled in some way. The other is whether we should be held responsible for our actions, whether praise or blame are in order. As I shall argue in a moment these two sorts of issue get run together and confused in ordinary common-sense thinking, so that questions of what I shall call metaphysical freedom get mixed up with questions of moral or legal responsibility.

A man confined in a prison cell is compelled to be so: he cannot get through the locked door or break down the stone walls He may want above all else to walk over green grass and under trees, but unfortunately he does not. He cannot, because no

'Ought', 'can', free will and responsibility

matter what he decides to do, he does not leave his cell. Contrast this with the case of a person enjoying a walk in the country. He or she does so freely, in the sense that he or she wants to do so and does do so. To say that he or she could do otherwise is to say that his or her doing so would be compatible with certain background assumptions about his or her circumstances and with the laws of nature. (If the person had not wanted to go for the walk he or she would not have done so.) The person who is enjoying a walk in the country is indeed being *caused* to do so by his desires and beliefs, but the person is not *compelled*.

If we all the time did what we most wanted to do, then, however deterministic the universe is, we would act freely, not under compulsion. Our actions would flow from our desires.

A woman may freely decide to have a surgical operation. She does what she most wants to do under the circumstances because though she does not like the idea of the operation, she likes still less the consequences of not having the operation. What she most wants to do is to do what she wants most to do out of a set of alternative actions set by the physical circumstances.

Now consider the case of a man who is carrying some money belonging to some charitable organization, and who is threatened by a robber. The robber says that he will shoot the man if the latter does not hand over the money. The man naturally does hand over the money to the robber. Other things being equal he would not want to hand over the money, but in this case he does want to hand it over, because this is the only way in which he can avoid being shot. Now since he is acting in accordance with his character, doing what he most wants to do out of all the physically possible alternatives open to him, should we not say that he is acting freely? Metaphysically I think that we should say that he *is* acting freely, in a sense in which free will is compatible with determinism. That is, a person is free if he or she could do otherwise, i.e. would have done otherwise if he or she had wanted to. If the man had wanted to be shot rather than hand over the money, then he would not have handed over the money.

There is, however, a tendency to say that the man threatened by the robber was coerced, and so not free. After all there is not much to be said for being held in a prison cell with an open door and an armed guard even though if one wanted to one could walk through and be shot! It is easy therefore to see how common sense regards the man threatened by the robber as *not* free. There is an oddity here. Suppose that the man threatened by the other was not carrying money but was a secret service agent. Suppose also that the man who threatened to shoot the first man was an enemy member of secret police who wanted by his threats to cause the agent to divulge the names of his colleagues, which would lead to the liquidation of these colleagues. We might still think of the threats coercing the man in the first case, but in the second case we tend to think more easily of this man having a free choice. We may think indeed that the agent ought to prefer death to divulging the information. There would be a difficult choice, which does not exist in the case of 'your money or your life'. We would not blame a man for giving up the money to the robber, even though it was not his money, whereas we might indeed blame (or even punish) the agent who divulged the names of his colleagues (even though one might feel sympathy for the agent's predicament and wonder whether one might oneself be brave enough to make the right choice in similar circumstances). And yet the two cases are exactly similar from the point of view of metaphysical freedom: in each case the agent who handed over the money or divulged the names of his colleagues was doing what in the circumstances he most wanted to do, and in each case he would have done otherwise if he had wanted otherwise.

It is easy to see, therefore, how metaphysical considerations about freedom (which I interpret as the ability to do what one most wants to do in the circumstances) get mixed up with questions of praise and blame, responsibility and reward. We would hold the man who divulged the names of his colleagues as responsible, because divulging these names leads to worse results than being shot. There may be a utility in censuring or punishing the agent who divulges the names of his colleagues: this will tend to encourage other agents to remain steadfast. There is no utility in censuring a person who gave a charity's bag of money to a robber, rather than be shot. This would be so even if the consequence of being shot were not that the robber got the money anyway. Unless the bag of money were of quite astronomical value it is likely that it would be better that the charity lose the money to the robber than that a human life be lost.

Bad results for which it is useful to hold people responsible need not be intended. A person may be negligent or reckless or just unlucky. Suppose that a man in a crowded street sees a friend a hundred yards further up the street and runs towards him, in order to catch the friend before he disappears and to have a beer with him. In so doing the man knocks over and seriously injures a child. We hold him responsible not because he intended to injure the child but because he was doing something that would very likely result in something of the sort. If the man knew about the probability of harm resulting we call him reckless. If he did not think of this but should have we call him negligent. In either case we hold him responsible, and there is obviously a social utility in doing so. Holding people responsible for negligent or reckless acts discourages reckless or negligent acts: it encourages people to worry more about probable unintended consequences if they know them, and it encourages people to think more beforehand.

Frank Jackson has elucidated our ascription of responsibility or blameworthiness in terms of consideration of what he calls 'expected moral utility'.[11] For a convinced utilitarian expected moral utility is just expected utility. Consider all the possible states of affairs, each stretching indefinitely into the future. Sum the products of the utility of each state (i.e. the strengths of the utilitarian's preferences for such states) and the subjective probability of the state and we get expected utility. However not all philosophers are utilitarians and common-sense morality is not utilitarian either. Common-sense morality depends also on preferences for such states of affairs as that of a moral rule being complied with. So Jackson generalizes the notion of expected utility to that of expected moral utility. Then he claims that we hold a person blameworthy if that person does not maximize expected moral utility. If the man running fast through the street had been trying to catch a terrorist, say, then the expected moral utility of his action would have been high, even though, as it turned out, he missed the terrorist and hurt a child. Things turned out badly, but the argument is probabilistic and we would advise anyone else to do the same thing on a similar occasion. (I am assuming that though the man missed the terrorist, the probability of his in fact catching the terrorist had indeed been a fairly high one.) In the case of negligence, as Jackson points out, the failure to act for which one is held blameworthy is that of failing to take thought about expected moral utility, and of course acts of taking thought about expected moral utility themselves have expected moral utility.

Let us go back to the case of the man who handed over the charity's money to the robber. We do not hold such a man responsible for losing the money because the expected moral utility of handing over the money is less than that of getting shot. The man makes a free choice and we applaud it. Our denial of responsibility is sufficiently explained without denial that the man is free. If we did hold that the man was not free we could get ourselves into a certain paradox. I have said that the man was free because he was doing what he most wanted to do (avoiding getting shot). Admittedly he would rather have kept the money *and* not be shot, but the situation made this impossible. If we were to say that the man who gave the money to save his life was doing what he did not want to do, why should we not say the same of a person who gave money to a starving family? If one was not free why was the other? Why is it commonly thought that the man threatened by the robber is coerced and not free, while the charitable person is free? One could say that the charitable person is coerced by the existence of the starving family, which acts on benevolence just as the sight of the robber's pistol acts on fear. We usually do not think of this. This is partly because the charitable person is not being intentionally coerced. (But nor do prison walls intentionally coerce. Perhaps the prison officers who keep the door locked intentionally coerce, but consider then the case of a man in a mine and imprisoned by a rock fall.) Of course the charitable act should be praised and not blamed. Otherwise, however, there is an interesting symmetry between the two cases. Possibly a relevant difference is that benevolence is not a feeling against which the ordinary good person feels a need to struggle. If he or she did so want to struggle he or she would not be a good person and he or she would be unlikely to help the starving family, whereas fear is something we normally have too much of, even though fear worked beneficially when the man was threatened by the robber.

If a person does not have the right preferences, then his or her expected utility will not be expected *moral* utility. If a person maximizes his or her own utility as determined by his or her overall preferences, he or she will not maximize expected moral utility. Hence according to Jackson's account, he or she will be held blameworthy. But what if a person's preferences diverge from moral ones because of some physical cause, such as a lesion in the brain? Common-sense morality tends to excuse in this case, and Jackson's theory (as Jackson recognizes) does not apply. It is not absolutely clear why or whether this ought to be so. Presumably burglars who would not have burglarious tendencies but for a lesion in the brain need to be deterred by social sanctions no less than those whose burglarious tendencies are due in some part to the genetic legacy of their parents. If a person could be burglarious because of post-hypnotic suggestion the same sort of thing might be said, but perhaps here it might be a question of deterring the hypnotist rather than the patient.

There is also a tendency not to hold that persons suffering from mental illness are responsible, or at least we tend to ascribe diminished responsibility. A kleptomaniac, for example, may be thought of as not free to resist stealing from a shop, the agoraphobic as not free to enjoy a walk in the country, the sex maniac as not free to avoid molesting women. Originally the idea may have been that of an indeterministic will or soul being thwarted by a defective animal nature, but be that as it may the determinist can in his own fashion go some way to justify the sort of distinction that is made by the law and by common morality. The determinist can argue that there is no utility in punishing kleptomaniacs because the threat of punishment will not deter the kleptomaniac from such behaviour, nor will the example of one kleptomaniac have a deterrent effect on other kleptomaniacs. In fact, inability to be influenced by threats or by reasonable argument as to the likely consequences of actions may be made the test of diminished responsibility. I do not mean to say that the distinctions that the ordinary man or the law makes here are indubitably rational ones. It is not completely obvious that leniency to the mentally ill has no deterrent effect: it depends on whether or not the sane are able to deceive court psychiatrists into thinking that they are not sane and so should be treated with leniency. Moreover even if a sex maniac is treated mercifully, there will still be good reasons for locking him up and not letting him loose to harm people.

I have drawn attention to the way in which questions of the rationality (or utility) of ascribing responsibility get mixed up in ordinary thought with what I referred to as metaphysical freedom. I now want to consider a fantastic case, which could not occur in practice, but which will illuminate the nature of ordinary conceptions of free will.

In this piece of futuristic fiction, let us suppose that a mad scientist could 're-programme' a person's brain. By altering the synaptic connections and changing whatever embodies the memory traces, the scientist changes a person from being a successful and happy poet so as to become an equally successful and happy engineer. As an engineer this person decides to design a certain sort of bridge. Was the person not free in doing so? According to the deterministic account of free will, the person was free because the action flowed from the person's desires and character generally. Suppose that the person was negligent in bridge designing, so that later the bridge fell down and caused deaths. It is a moot question how much common sense would hold the person responsible. And if not, why not? But as I have said, common sense runs together the questions of metaphysical freedom and of ascription of responsibility. Separating them, let us consider the question of metaphysical freedom. The determinist would surely need to say that the engineer's act was free, in that if the engineer had not wanted to do the act the engineer would not have done it. This consideration makes me think that quite apart from the question of responsibility the determinist's account of free will can do no more than approximate to the common-sense one. That is, it can give the same answer as common sense would give in many practical applications, but it can never coincide with common sense, because common-sense discourse about free will is not always consistent.

These considerations suggest, then, that even for a theory of metaphysical freedom, let alone for justifying ascriptions of responsibility, determinism does not give us *quite* what common sense wants. Let us consider the theory that free will requires indeterminism. This leads us to consider the second horn of the dilemma that I posed earlier in this chapter.

DISCUSSION OF SUB-ARGUMENT (2)

Sub-argument (2) considered what we should say if we thought

'Ought', 'can', free will and responsibility

that our actions were the outcome of pure chance, the sort of chance that we get in quantum mechanics. This is to be contrasted with the ordinary sort of chance that is compatible with determinism, namely the unusual intersection of two causal chains. (See Aristotle, *Physics*, 196b-197b.) A man is cycling along the road to buy a newspaper and he is hit on the head by a falling branch. There are no laws or good generalizations relating cyclings to buy newspapers with hittings on heads by falling branches. On the other hand, in Canberra it is common in the spring time to be swooped on by Australian magpies: if one cycles near a nesting magpie one can expect to be hit on the head by its beak. This is not chance, because there are good generalizations about the behaviour of nesting magpies. The contrast between chance or accident here and not chance is consistent with determinism. Sub-argument (2) mentions pure chance, not the just-mentioned weak or Aristotelian sort of chance.

According to this sub-argument, if our choices are not determined but just pop out of the blue by pure chance, they cannot be an instance of free choice. The combination of sub-arguments (1) and (2) suggests that whether we are determined or act by pure chance we are not free. C.A. Campbell, in a very interesting attempt to defend the anti-determinist (or 'libertarian') position, has argued that the alternatives of 'determinism' and 'pure chance' are not the only ones. Another alternative to determinism, he believes, is acting by 'contra-causal freedom'. Such freedom, he holds, is indeterministic but is not chance.[12]

If contra-causal freedom is indeterministic, however, there is the problem that there is a good deal of predictability in human action, as David Hume pointed out in his *Treatise*, Book II, Part 3, Section 1 and in his *Inquiry*, Section 8, Part 1. If we could not be reasonably sure, on most occasions, how other people were likely to behave, social life would be impossible. So also would be the conjectures of historians. Campbell has an answer here. At the cost of restricting the application of the concept 'free' much more narrowly than one would unreflectively be inclined to do, or than a determinist such as Hobart would reflectively do, Campbell holds that contra-causal freedom occurs only in those cases in which we act out of sense of duty against our strongest desire. (Here, of course, he is reminiscent of Kant.) Such exercises of willpower are relatively uncommon, because our inclinations and our duty most often do not conflict. Campbell is thus able to come to terms with the general predictability of human actions.

Of course a naturalistically minded person will be puzzled by the treatment of sense of duty as different in kind from all other desires. Our desire to do our duty is readily explicable as a result of social conditioning, and there is nothing in it that a determinist cannot allow. Surely the reason why we say that desire A is stronger than desire B is that it is desire A and not desire B that issues in action. If our sense of duty issues in our doing A, even though we otherwise most want to do B, then the desire to do B cannot be our strongest desire.

Clearly Campbell does not think of acting from contra-causal freedom as acting from a desire. But then his term 'contra-causal freedom' needs to be explained to us. He does so by inviting us to reflect introspectively on actions in which we, as he thinks, act against our strongest desire. When we so introspect, he thinks, we see 'genuinely open possibilities'. Now no doubt we may say to ourselves 'I can do this and I can do that'. The notion of possibility is relative to background assumptions. Suppose I am climbing a mountain and I dislodge a rock, which falls and narrowly misses the head of a companion. I say to myself 'It could have killed him'. What I mean (to put the matter a little misleadingly in terms of 'possible worlds') is that if the initial conditions had been slightly different in certain ways, that is in a certain 'possible world' very like the actual world and with the same laws of nature, then the counterpart in that world of the rock crashes into the counterpart of my companion. Here contextual considerations indicate what conditions are to be held fixed, and certainly the laws of nature are held fixed. On the other hand if one wonders what could happen in a universe with different laws of nature, then it is things other than the law of nature that are held fixed or as nearly as possible fixed. Sometimes the context may indicate that if we say that something could happen we are merely saying that the sentence asserting that the thing in question happens is merely consistent with the laws of logic. Again, if I have the appropriate railway ticket I can travel on a certain train: in doing so I am not breaking any regulation of the railways. A possible world in which a counterpart of me travels on a counterpart of the train is one in which no such regulation is broken. There are all sorts of contexts and appropriate sorts of possibility.

Suppose I do a certain action and say that I could have done otherwise. What I mean is that doing otherwise is not incompatible with the laws of nature, and not incompatible with the state of my brain being within a certain range of possible states. To say that the falling rock could have hit my companion is to say that if the initial conditions (the way in which and the time at which I disturbed it) had been only slightly different in some definite way then the rock would have hit my companion. If I drop a china plate and it does not break, I may say that it could have broken – if the initial conditions had been slightly different in a certain way then it would have broken. If I drop an aluminium plate I may say: 'It not only did not break but it could not have broken. *However* I had dropped it the plate would not have broken.'

Campbell, however, wants to hold not only the laws of nature fixed but also the initial conditions. And if this is the contextual presupposition then of course neither I nor the rock can do otherwise. The determinist will not be worried by this, because he or she will say that this is not the relevant presupposition when in cases of practical importance we use the expression 'could have done otherwise'. The kleptomaniac could not do otherwise than steal in the sense that if the initial conditions had included further threats or means of detection he would still have stolen. The ordinary thief, in contrast, would not steal if the threats and certainty of detection were greater. Again, sometimes I may say 'I could have done otherwise' meaning 'If I had wanted to I would have done otherwise'. Here the important initial conditions that are varied would include my desires.

Thus the determinist can point to contextual presumptions that make his or her uses of 'could have done otherwise' perfectly sensible. The determinist also will think that there is an unclarity in the libertarian's position. He or she will agree that if an action happened by pure chance then the initial conditions *and* the laws of nature could be the same and yet the action could be different. (So also, as the libertarian will say, if the action happened not by pure chance but by 'contra-causal freedom'.)

Campbell thinks that we can discover the meaning of 'contra-causal freedom' by means of introspection: we introspect in a situation in which sense of duty conflicts with our strongest desire. He thinks that we then see that (absolutely) we can do one thing and we can do another. But it is not clear to me what is meant here, over and above what the determinist could allow. Campbell does not mean that it is 'pure chance' that he should do one thing or do the other thing. He can introspect that he says to himself 'I can do this and I can do that', but this gets us no further into understanding a libertarian interpretation of what is said.

I would argue that the libertarian theory of free will is implausible in the light of a biological view of man. It is hard to see how a libertarian free will could arise by mutation and natural selection. We can see in principle how a change in a DNA molecule could lead to a change in the innate structure of a brain, but how could it cause the sort of non-physical entity that a libertarian (contra-causal) free will would be? However this deserves to be discussed at length elsewhere than in a book mainly on meta-ethics. There is the additional problem that Campbell's explication of 'pure chance' would seem to depend on an obscure and at any rate implausible philosophy of language. Since Wittgenstein we have learned that meanings are not objects of introspection, and it is unclear to me how introspection could help us to understand the notion of 'contra-causal freedom'.[13]

SOME QUESTIONS ABOUT PLAUSIBILITY

I have taken the view that the human nervous system behaves near enough as a deterministic system. Neurons are macroscopic objects whose behaviour must be understood electro-chemically and quantum-mechanical indeterminacy is not relevant. Furthermore, as D.M. MacKay has contended,[14] there is much redundancy in the nervous system, which has evolved in such a way as to function well with faulty components, so that an action will depend on the mass behaviour of very many neurons and any indeterminacy which might apply to the functioning of only a handful of neurons would not affect matters.

Sir John Eccles has defended a dualistic theory. According to him the mind is something which exists in addition to the brain:

his theory is very similar to Cartesian dualism. In his joint book with Sir Karl Popper, *The Self and its Brain*, he suggests that the interaction of the brain with what he calls 'the self-conscious mind' is due to modules of neurons, such as are known anatomically, each consisting of thousands of neurons organized rather in the way an electronic micro-circuit is, but in a much more complicated way.[15] It looks as though he holds that contemporary physics is incomplete even as regards 'ordinary matter'. Following the physicist Gerald Feinberg[16] I suggest on the contrary that in application to 'ordinary matter' (of which neurons, etc. consist) modern physics shows all the signs of being complete. We are not in the position, say, of a Newtonian cosmology which cannot deal with electric forces and so cannot explain well known phenomena of bulk matter. According to Feinberg if we neglect transitory particles that are created only at very high energies, and cosmological matters, such as the interiors of neutron stars or of black holes, physics is essentially complete – Thales's problem of the nature of ordinary bulk matter has been solved. To understand ordinary matter the physics of the electron, proton, photon and neutrino suffices. *A fortiori* revolutionary discoveries in physics are unlikely to affect chemistry or our understanding of living cells, such as neurons. Therefore it could be argued, contrary to Eccles, that for the purpose of discussing the mind-body problem, free will, and the brain generally, present day physics will suffice.

According to Eccles's view, not only would immaterial minds exist, but there would have to be forces of interaction between the immaterial mind and its brain: it presumably would be the function of a module to 'tune into' these forces, just as a radio receiver tunes into electro-magnetic forces. But would not the whole problem recur again? Are the actions of the immaterial mind determined by its earlier states, or do they occur by pure chance? In either case is the immaterial mind free? Or is the mind supposed to act by contra-causal freedom? But it is not any easier to make sense of this in a mentalistic context than it was in a materialistic one. And if the immaterial mind could be free though determined why should not the material mind equally well be free though determined? Eccles has been much influenced by the philosophical views of Sir Karl Popper. Popper's polemic against materialism and determinism relies heavily on his doctrine of three worlds, 'World 1', 'World 2' and 'World 3',[17] but I find this doctrine hard to understand, particularly as it relates to 'World 3', which seems to be both Platonically eternal *and* a creation of the human mind. Popper's speculations about World 3 suggest the possibility of interpreting him as saying that a free action is determined not by causes in time but by non-temporal World 3 entities (logical principles, etc.). But then if these eternal entities did determine our actions this would have to be via triggering events in time, and so surely the actions would still be caused.[18]

The idea that the will can be moved acausally may be connected with a contextual ambiguity in the question 'What was your reason?' (for travelling to Scotland, for example). One answer might be to say 'I wanted to see my aunt'. Here I am mentioning a desire, and giving a causal explanation (or part explanation). Another might be 'My aunt lives in Scotland'. Here this might be elliptical for 'I believe that my aunt lives in Scotland'. In this case one would still be giving a causal answer, since beliefs as well as desires are part causes of actions. On the other hand, if 'My aunt lives in Scotland' is taken as on its own, it is taken as giving a justificatory, rather than a causal answer. Though I am not mentioning a proposition I am presenting one by asserting it. If such a justificatory answer were confused with a causal one then it could be half thought that propositions influence our actions without causing them. This feeling might be particularly strong, perhaps, if the proposition presented were a principle of logic. I present this suggestion for what it is worth.

CONCLUSION ABOUT FREE-WILL AND DETERMINISM

The determinist, or determinist at the macroscopic level, can regard the human mind as a deterministic mechanism and can yet present us with a concept of free will that makes at least very many of the practically important distinctions that the ordinary man and the law make by means of talk about free will. If this deterministic notion does not fit in with some of the things the ordinary man (or even the law) also wants to say, this does not matter too much. The ordinary man may have an *inconsistent* concept of free will, making it at one and the same time both deterministic (so that actions flow from character) and indeterministic. If so it is not surprising that a clear philosophical account of the issues does not legitimize *exactly* the ordinary man's range of distinctions between 'free' and 'not free'.

Thus we can say *either* that we are not free but that this does not matter for morality or the law, *or* that we are free but that this is compatible with determinism. Which we say will depend on how much we put into the concept of free will (i.e. on the range of the sentences of the form 'A man is free only if . . .' to which we assent). Indeed if we put so much into the concept as to make it inconsistent we end up by putting everything in, since an inconsistent proposition enables us to deduce any proposition whatever.

VIII

ETHICS, SCIENCE AND METAPHYSICS

PROGRESS IN ETHICS v. PROGRESS IN SCIENCE

It has frequently been lamented that while the human species has made immense progress in science it is nevertheless ethically backward. This ethical backwardness is all the more dangerous because the advanced state of scientific knowledge has made available a technology with which we are able to destroy ourselves – indeed a technology which may have got so much out of hand we may not even have the capacity to prevent it from destroying us.

If what is meant by this is that many of our desires and emotions are inappropriate to the present state of civilization, then this lament about the dangerous backwardness of ethics is obviously justified. Nevertheless I believe that there are several confusions in the way in which the backwardness of ethics is commonly contrasted with the advanced state of science.

The notion of progress in ethics is an ambiguous one. When we are talking of progress in ethics we may be concerned with progress towards a more perfect system of ethical *precepts*. We might, however, be thinking of a different sort of progress: namely towards a more perfect conformity by the generality of mankind to some given set of precepts. Let us call progress towards more perfect systems of ethical precepts by the name 'progress in ethics', and let us reserve the term 'progress in morality' for progress towards a more general observance of some given set of precepts. Then, once we have made this distinction, the comparison between the backward state of ethics and morality as compared with the advanced state of science becomes less striking. We need to make a similar distinction in the case of science. Corresponding to progress in ethics we need to distinguish progress towards more and more adequate scientific theories, and corresponding to progress in morality we need to distinguish progress towards a more generally scientific way of thought in society generally.

Let us take the question of progress in ethics first. Because of the inevitable subjectivity in ethics that I have attempted to bring out in previous chapters, I here speak for myself and not necessarily the reader, but a reader whose ultimate preferences are not too different from mine may be willing to go along with me. One reason why we might not have too much progress in ethics could be that we have already got a perfect or near-perfect set of ethical precepts, perhaps the Golden Rule of the New Testament. (I interpret the Golden Rule as some form of utilitarianism, which is based on the sentiment of generalized benevolence, but for the purpose of the present chapter I do not wish to insist on this precise interpretation.) Not only is it the case that there have been people who have accepted these precepts, or something like them, in the sense of assenting to them, but there have been saintly people who have regularly acted in accordance with them.

One way in which there has indeed been progress in ethics recently has been through the realization by some ethicists that animal happiness and suffering has to be considered equally with that of human beings. I should draw attention here to the remarkable book *Animal Liberation* by Peter Singer.[1] Christian ethics has been deficient in this respect, since animals have been regarded as things made by God for the use of men. Even St Francis has a not too clear record on this question. If we are to believe the tradition (but perhaps we should not take this as good historical evidence), one of his disciples cut a trotter off a living pig to give to another of the brethren who was ill. St Francis told the disciple to apologize to the owner of the pig, not for his cruelty but for having damaged the property.[2] However, utilitarianism has been mindful of animals. Unlike Kantians, who are primarily concerned with the rationality of those with whom we deal, Bentham, for example, was clear that the important

Ethics, science and metaphysics

question was not whether animals are rational, but was whether they can suffer.[3] At any rate, the increased attention to the sufferings of animals is one of the most notable examples of progress in ethics over the last hundred years or so. We should, of course, be equally mindful of extra-terrestrial consciousnesses, should we come across any such and have to interact with them.

I am not denying that there are practically important controversial areas in ethics, such as in the abortion debate, and perhaps most importantly, about nuclear war. Sometimes the differences here may turn at least partly on scientific fact, but as I shall suggest later, they may turn on metaphysical differences. I do not want myself to draw a sharp line between metaphysics and science,[4] but even those who do will presumably put metaphysics, like science, on the 'belief' side of the belief/desire dichotomy. Nevertheless the area of moral disagreement should not be exaggerated too much. One may sincerely accept good ethical precepts and yet fail to apply them. Such failures may be really a failure in science, not in ethics. That is, we may act wrongly not because we are not mindful of a good ethical precept but because we lack the empirical knowledge to apply this precept in the particular case. Thus physicians used to kill off their patients instead of curing them, not because they did not wish to do as they would be done by, but because they falsely thought that bleedings, purges and other horrifying treatments did in fact have the effect of curing diseased people. Similarly, consider the case of a benevolent statesman who nevertheless causes poverty and unemployment because he is incompetent in economics, or because he is in a sense competent but no workable economic theory has been devised by the experts. Consider again planners who are unable to appreciate exponential growth and population explosions in the absence of family planning. Indeed some of these issues may give rise to intractable problems, however benevolent, competent, and well-advised statesmen and planners may be: the problems may be analogous to intractable problems in technology. Consider the difficulty in devising ways of harnessing fusion power to peaceful use. Consider again the arms race. The great powers have got themselves into a game-theoretic situation (which admittedly if statesmen on both sides had been of better will thirty or more years ago they might not have put us into) such that it is not completely obvious that ways of breaking the deadlock can be devised even granted good will on both sides.

Thus many failures to apply good ethical precepts can be put down to failure in applied science rather than to failure in ethics as such. Nevertheless it is also the case that very many people do not accept good ethical precepts, but accept maleficent ethical systems. People are often motivated by religious fanaticism, political ideologies, and so on, and are thus driven by motives quite other than those of generalized benevolence. Now in this respect ethics is not all that different from science. The credulity of the majority of human beings is immense. In one Australian university, at the beginning of an academic year when students were advertising their various clubs and societies, I once noticed a table manned by members of an astrology society. I felt distressed that such credulity could exist even among university students. If there are maleficent systems of ethics in the world today so also there are ridiculous but influential systems of factual belief. The decline of orthodox religion has by no means caused a decline in superstition: when one devil goes out seven more rush in to take its place.

PROGRESS IN MORALITY

Let us now pass from the question of progress in ethics to that of progress in morality as I have defined this phrase. It must be admitted that there are a lot of selfish, fanatical or wicked people in the world today who are insensitive to human misery or who even rejoice in cruelty. However in many countries there does appear to have been a considerable advance in beneficent and humane feeling. It is hard to imagine a resurgence of bear baiting, dog fighting, public executions, and so on, in a country such as Britain or Australia. Nevertheless, terrible things are done in wars, and though it is hard to imagine something like the extermination of the Tasmanian aborigines occurring nowadays it is possible that if the aborigines had been more numerous and necessary for our economic development Australia could easily have found itself with a social structure like that of South Africa. The recent events in Kampuchea under Pol Pot, among many others, show how little human beings may behave in accordance with an acceptable system of ethical precepts. Perhaps it will be said that in these cases they do not even pay lip service to these precepts and that they are carried away by ideology, so that the trouble lies in their ethics, not their morality, as I have defined these terms. However, I suspect that often ideology is a mere excuse. Thus I suspect that terrorists who contend that their terrorism is merely an unfortunately necessary means to a good ideological end may well be deluding themselves, and that in many cases what they particularly enjoy is the mayhem of terrorism itself, and that any ideology that seemed to provide an excuse for it would thereby gain in attractiveness.

We may suppose, therefore, that the morality of the generality of mankind is not very high. Most of even the nice people are rather selfish. Most of us in such countries as Australia and Britain like to live our comfortable suburban lives without thinking much of the privations of those in the poor countries. We blind ourselves to overseas miseries just as the upper class people in Victorian Britain blinded themselves to the privations of the poor workers in industry, agriculture and domestic service. Nevertheless the world does contain a sizeable minority of highly beneficent, self-sacrificing and even saintly people. Most of us could name some of these among our acquaintances, and there are of course the outstanding ones, such as Mother Teresa. These last correspond to scientists like Einstein and Dirac: one should not expect the world to contain too many of them. Just as saintly people are in a small minority, so also are great scientists. (Indeed if the minority were not a small one we should not talk in terms of saintliness or greatness.)

We may add to this the reflection that if even the people who are highly moral, though falling short of saintliness, are in a minority too, though not such a small one, the same may be said of scientists. If we think not of geniuses such as Einstein and Dirac but of the community of scientists generally, including such people as the bulk of professional officers in research organizations, lecturers in universities and technical colleges, and so on, we are still concerned with very much a minority of human beings in the world today. They are surely outweighed by the superstitious and irrational majority. (We must remember also that even a scientist can be superstitious and irrational: he can have a compartmented mind.) It is true that there are probably about as many scientists alive today as in the whole previous history of the human species, but this is partly (though not wholly) because there are about as many people alive today as in the whole previous history of humanity. Thus if progress in science is judged by the progress in scientific rationality among the *generality* of men and women it may not seem so great. More usually we think of progress in science as measured by the progress of a scientific elite in discovering new phenomena and devising new and better explanations. Our judgment of the progress of science is not affected by the consideration that the generality of men and women are unsympathetic to or ignorant of scientific methodology and scientific explanations. The scientific community has found a way of insulating itself from the irrational majority and of preventing itself from being harmed by it. (Such insulation has of course sometimes been ineffective, as is shown by cases such as those of Galileo and the Inquisition and of Soviet geneticists and Lysenko.)

If progress in science is judged by the work of an elite minority of the human race, why should not progress in morality be judged by the progress of a moral elite? The difference presumably is that the existence of a superstitious or irrational majority does not do much harm to scientists, but the existence of a wicked, selfish or fanatical majority is of course highly harmful to the general level of morality, and is threatening also to the more moral members of society themselves.

Let us therefore think of those who we regard as the more moral members of society as a moral elite, much as the generality of scientists form a scientific elite. Who we regard as a moral elite of course depends on our desires or attitudes (e.g. benevolence, love of fairness, respect for persons) but however much my readers and I may differ in these respects I hope that I can assume enough agreement in roughly agreeing to a great extent on who would go into the moral elite. I hope I do not need to stress that such a moral elite must not be confused with a social or intellectual elite. Many people of no great education and of no prestigious social position certainly belong to my envisaged moral elite. If we judge this moral elite by its adherence to something like the Golden Rule of the New Testament, there is not all that much room for its improvement. One place in which it could be improved is, as I suggested earlier, the extension of our moral

Ethics, science and metaphysics

sympathies to non-human animals. This last implies of course an improvement in ethics, as opposed to morality, as I have defined it, unless we already understand 'Do as you would be done by' as applicable to whales, cattle, chickens, and so on, as it is to human beings. Of course fully to understand what this injunction comes to we need to take into account theories about the degrees of consciousness that various creatures possess. I would suppose that the consciousness of whales is comparable to ours, that of chickens very different, and that of lizards very conjectural. When our philosophical and scientific knowledge of minds is greater we may be able to improve on our estimates. Of course even though they may not have the capacity for happiness and suffering that whales have, nevertheless I would suppose that chickens can suffer quite a lot, even though their consciousness should be very much a sort of daze, and this should be taken into account in our dealings with them. Perhaps in order to qualify for a moral elite one should become a heroic vegetarian like Peter Singer. I am myself not so heroic. I eat eggs though they may come from battery hens. Moreover at present I see no moral objection to eating the flesh of *free range* cattle, which seem to me to have a happy life which they would not have at all if they were not destined to be eaten. But this is a digression and I must return to my main theme.

ETHICS AND RHETORIC

I have argued that in an open society questions of ultimate principle depend on our preferences or desires, 'how we feel'. Let me illustrate this by the dispute about the utilitarian principle that one always ought so to act as to maximize the total happiness of all sentient beings. Utilitarianism has been contested by philosophers who feel that the principle of maximizing happiness needs to be supplemented by a principle of justice. Unfortunately the universe is so constituted that sometimes the only way in which we can increase the *total* happiness is by reducing the happiness of some minority. Though I am strongly inclined to advocate utilitarianism I cannot but be moved by the following beautiful words of William James, from his book *The Will to Believe*:

Or if the hypothesis were offered us of a world in which Messrs Fourier's and Bellamy's and Morris's utopias should all be outdone, and millions kept permanently happy on the one simple condition that a certain lost soul on the far-off edge of things should lead a life of lonely torture, what except a specifical and independent sort of emotion can it be which would make us immediately feel, even though an impulse arose within us to clutch at the happiness so offered, how hideous a thing would be its enjoyment when deliberately accepted as the fruit of such a bargain.[5]

These words of William James provide a moving account of why many people find utilitarianism repugnant, and wish to modify it at least by some principle of equal distribution. I think that we can put aside as irrelevant the consideration that since in our present non-utopian world very many souls are already in lonely torture, James's bargain might actually reduce the number of such tortured souls. We can suppose this outweighed by the supposition that the soul on the far-off edge of things lives an infinitely long life, and that all other tortured souls are finite in number and finite in life span. Alternatively we can suppose that James's bargain is proposed to us as inhabitants of a universe in which there is no actual pain, though no great positive happiness, so that the bargain would not reduce the number of souls already in lonely torture: it would merely produce (except for the one lonely soul) a life of rapturous happiness. Perhaps it might be said that happiness and torture are incommensurable, so that no amount of happiness can outweigh a given amount of torture, even though they belong to the same person. This does not seem plausible because we are often willing to trade pain for happiness. An obvious case is that of willingness to trade the pains of broken bones for sporting enjoyment. So the issue does come down to whether just distribution of happiness should be an independent moral principle.

I do not want to try to settle the dispute between James and the utilitarian here. I think that James's reference to a 'specifical and independent sort of emotion' is a red herring: the utilitarian's feeling of generalized benevolence, his desire for a maximization of the happiness of all sentient beings, is not 'specifical' or 'independent' any more than is James's feeling for justice. The way we feel in this sort of case may depend on the way we feel about personal identity.[6] Those who have a strong view of the unity of a person may think that the case of sacrificing one temporal stage of oneself for the benefit of a later stage (as when we go to the dentist or undergo a surgical operation) is relevantly different from that of sacrificing one person for the greater good of others, whereas those who have a more Humean view of personality (or similarly non-unitary views in terms of modern neurophysiology) may not feel this so strongly. It could possibly be the case that James appeals to egoistic feelings in us. It is possible that no one would be so altruistic as to consent to be the lonely tortured soul himself, however great the millennium he might help to achieve by this bargain. But if so, on reading James's words, we may feel that if they appeal to covert egoism, perhaps there is much to be said for egoism.

Utilitarians appeal ultimately to generalized benevolence. Many other moralists would rest their systems at least *partly* on an appeal to this feeling. Considerations of genetics and sociobiology suggest ways in which an innate tendency to a limited benevolence towards family or tribe might have arisen in us. Possibly a universal benevolence is developed out of more limited benevolence by analogy with a generalizing tendency that has worked well in science and in various types of pre-scientific thought. Thus concern for family, tribe and nation gets extended to a concern for all humanity, to all sentient beings on earth, including the non-human animals, and finally perhaps to all sentient beings, including extra-terrestrial ones, if we should ever come across them.[7]

On such lines as these we might try to explain the feeling of generalized benevolence. However to explain is not to justify. Why should we prefer the attitudes of Socrates to those of Hitler? It would appear that *ultimate* ethical attitudes cannot be justified because such a justification would have to be in terms of showing that these attitudes subserved further attitudes, in which case the supposedly ultimate attitudes would not be ultimate after all.

If two people agree in ultimate attitudes they may disagree in subordinate attitudes because of disagreements about cause and effect, and hence a dispute between them may be resolved on the level of scientific fact. Indeed sometimes disagreement in ultimate attitudes need not prevent two people from resolving their disagreement on factual grounds. Suppose that they disagree about ultimate ends, one person favouring ultimate end *A* and another favouring ultimate end *B*. However in a particular context something *C* may lead both to *A* and *B*. Then the two persons may discuss ways and means of achieving *C*. On the other hand disagreements in ultimate attitudes themselves cannot be resolved in this sort of way by means of factual discussion, and attempts to resolve them will be rhetorical in nature.

More often an ethical dispute will involve a mixture of rhetoric and factual reasoning. Consider the following example. In his autobiographical novel *Lavengro* George Borrow relates how, when he was fishing on the bank of a Norfolk river, a benevolent Quaker businessman came up and upbraided him for catching fish purely for sport, when he did not need them for food. The Quaker was dressed in a beaver hat. Borrow could have, but did not, ask the Quaker whether he was inconsistent in saying this and yet wearing a hat made from the skin of beavers, especially as beavers are highly developed mammals, with presumably much greater sensitivity and capacity for suffering than fish have. The Quaker might have replied that the beavers were not killed for sport but because their skins were useful for making hats. He might have used a theological premiss that fish and beavers were made by God for our use. Borrow could then have attacked this theological premiss on factual grounds, by arguing against the geocentric and anthropocentric cosmology that made such a view plausible. (If he had lived a little later in the nineteenth century he could have attacked the implied theory of special creation by citing the Darwinian theory of natural selection.) He might, if he had been a different sort of man, have urged metaphysical arguments against the existence of God. He could also have asked whether the pain and discomfort that the Quaker might suffer through not wearing a beaver hat was as great as the deprivation of happiness to the beavers when they were killed. The Quaker might have come round to arguing on these grounds, but might have contended that his not buying a beaver hat would not have saved the life of a single beaver, since demand outran supply. And so the argument could have gone on with a mixture of factual discourse and of rhetoric until the proponents had settled down into a stable position either of moral

Ethics, science and metaphysics

agreement or of moral disagreement.

Not all ethical arguments depend on such an admixture of rhetoric. As was suggested in Chapter 3 much ethical discourse could be carried out by making purely factual remarks, so as to canalize our audience's desires in preferred ways. It must be conceded also that rhetoric has its place in science too: at least we appeal to likings for simplicity and elegance in theories. Nevertheless the ultimate concern is for truth: we prize elegance and simplicity not only for practical or aesthetic reasons but because we think (however hard it is to justify this thought) that simplicity and elegance are a guide to truth. Even when it is for mere convenience that we prefer one theory to another equally consonant with the observed facts, there is still the question of the metaphysical truth of the preferred theory. Either the universe is (or is approximately) as the theory says it is or it is not.[8]

It may also be conceded that a dispute between a scientist and a pseudo-scientist may have all the intractability of an ultimate ethical dispute, since the scientist and the pseudo-scientist may accept different methodological principles.[9] Morality may come into it too, since the arguments of pseudo-scientists are often characterized by a lack of intellectual humility that is needed by even otherwise arrogant orthodox scientists. (One just does not get on in the scientific world without a certain sort of intellectual humility.) Nevertheless to a very great extent science is under control by the actual world. The scientist makes an atomic bomb, an antibiotic, or a communications satellite, whereas the pseudo-scientist cannot rub our noses in such obvious practicality. His supposed perpetual motion machines never work.

ETHICS AND METAPHYSICS

As I have remarked, I hold that metaphysics is continuous with science. As science gets more general and abstract it gets more metaphysical. Metaphysics, as I see it, is a search for the most plausible theory of the whole universe, as it is considered in the light of total science. In order to put the various sciences together much conceptual clarification is needed, but conceptual clarification is needed within science too. Thus elementary particle physics is more 'conceptual' than organic chemistry. Organic chemistry is difficult and highly sophisticated, but its problems are not conceptual in nature. They do not raise questions comparable to those of realism versus anti-realism, whether there must be action at a distance, and so on, such as we find in theoretical physics.[10]

On this view, therefore, metaphysics just is science – it is at one end of the scientific spectrum. Nevertheless I do not want to argue this point here. What I have to say below will not depend crucially on this assimilation of metaphysics to science – hence the sub-heading above 'Ethics and metaphysics', which should be read as neutral as to whether it could or could not be subsumed under 'Ethics and science'.

I want to illustrate the relevance of metaphysics to ethics by reference to what is the greatest moral problem that has ever faced the human race: the question of nuclear war. Perhaps the reader may think this odd of me, because the dangers of nuclear war are surely far too obvious to require metaphysics to show them off. Nevertheless I shall show a respect in which the wrong metaphysical outlook might cloud the issues. Certainly the main objections to nuclear war are obvious enough and what is needed is some way to stop and then reverse the arms race. Presumably neither metaphysicians nor natural scientists can do very much to tell us how to go about this: what is needed (if anything will do the trick) are new ideas in political theory and decision theory (in addition, of course, to a good understanding of the motives and actions and reactions of statesmen, which may come from an intelligent reading of history). Nevertheless I believe that metaphysical confusion can affect the direction of more down-to-earth discussions of the subject.

H.J. Groenewold has usefully distinguished between micro effects, meso effects and macro effects.[11] Traditional ethical thinking has been concerned mainly with micro effects of action, that is effects on small groups in small areas. The pace of change of the human and animal environment has in past centuries been slow. In this century meso effects have come to the fore, for example pollution of the environment, which may ultimately endanger whole populations, but not all human and animal life on earth. Now also, unfortunately, the threat of nuclear war makes us envisage macro effects (effects on all people and the whole earth): the end of the human race, perhaps also of mammalian life itself, and the end of the prospect of humans evolving into yet higher and more wonderful forms of life.[12] Traditional rules of ethical thinking were evolved in relation to micro effects and may be inappropriate. Certain philosophical systems of ethical precepts (and here I think particularly of utilitarianism) should be able to cope in theory with effects at any level, but even so their practical application is difficult because of the difficulties in envisaging consequences of rapid technological change.

One rule that Groenewold holds to be out of place when we are concerned with macro effects is that it is sane to think of probabilities but mad to think of mere possibilities (a view he attributes to Erich Fromm). What we ordinarily think of as a mere possibility is in fact a very low probability, but a very low probability multiplied by a macro disaster can still have macro disvalue. Those who comfort themselves with the thought that mutual deterrence has kept the peace for thirty years forget the importance of low probabilities in the macro context. Indeed what does it matter, from the perspective of possible millions of years of future evolution, that final catastrophe should merely be postponed for (say) a couple of hundred years? Postponing is only of great value if it is used as a breathing space in which ways are found to avert the final disaster. And even a small probability that we shall not have this breathing space will yield negative expected utility of macro dimensions.

This naturally leads me to consideration of a way in which metaphysical confusion can distort thinking on these matters. Most people's temporal horizons are limited. They find it hard to think of the arms race in relation to the millions of years of possible evolution of the human race that lie ahead if we do not destroy ourselves. Now I am inclined to think that this is partly because a lot of people do not believe in the reality of the future (and often also of the past). I recently heard an intelligent lecture on a non-philosophical theme by someone who began by saying, as though it were an obvious fact (instead of, as I think, an unintelligible metaphysical paradox), that only the knife edge of the present is real and that the past and future are mere mental constructions. I wonder whether his deceased great-grandfather would have relished the thought that he was one day to be described as a mere mental construction, and I wonder whether his great-grandchildren (if he has any) would relish the thought that their great-grandfather had questioned their reality.

I hold that there are all sorts of good philosophical reasons for believing in the reality of the future, but as I am at present concerned with meta-ethics and not with metaphysics I shall not go into the matter here.[13] And of course most people do plan for their own futures and for the futures of their children, and so disbelief in the reality of the future is not quite pervasive. Nevertheless I have observed that there is a good deal of this sort of disbelief mixed up with the thinking of non-philosophers, and some philosophers too. In so far as it exists it can be highly dangerous to the way in which we think of macro effects.

A strong feeling for the reality of the future, and of the possible glories of future evolution, would do much to dispel equanimity about the possible extinction of the human race. I should like here also to refer to another cause of such equanimity, which can be a concern with the abolition of suffering but not with the promotion of happiness. In a discussion of Groenewold's remarks, Hermann Vetter[14] says that he does not think that the extinction of the human race is one of the greatest evils with which we could be confronted, provided that this could be done instantaneously and painlessly.[15] Certainly there would be no future suffering on earth if all life on earth ceased.[16] But most people seem glad that they were born: we do not usually think of present people (and animals) that the pain in their lives outweighs their pleasures (though this may be far from the case with many destitute people in Third World countries[17]). There have been great advances in the human condition due to science: recollect the horrors of childbirth, surgical operations, even of having a tooth out, a hundred years ago. If the human race is not extinguished there may be cures of cancer, senility, and other evils, so that happiness may outweigh unhappiness in the case of more and more individuals. Perhaps our far superior descendants of a million years hence (if they exist) will be possessed of a felicity unimaginable to us. However I detect in Vetter's views a more questionable strain of thought. This is that if no one exists any longer there is no subject who we deprive of felicity. Vetter says that he does not think that we have moral duties towards unborn humans. Now if the unborn never come to exist there are no future entities towards which we can have duties. (Though if they do come to exist, why could we not have duties to them? Perhaps deontological ethics is here mixed up with worries about the reality of the future.) Perhaps there is a real conflict here between deontological ethics (expressed in terms of 'duties towards') and utilitarianism (expressed in terms of 'consequences of actions'). Perhaps there really is more need for progress in ethics than I suggested earlier in this chapter, namely more advocacy of utilitarianism. But here I stray from meta-ethics into normative ethics.

I have suggested here that clarity about the reality of the future is important for ethics, and hence that metaphysical beliefs can canalize our desires no less than scientific ones. Other areas in which metaphysics is relevant to ethics will occur to the reader. An obvious one is in discussion of contraception and of abortion. Opposition to these practices often (but not always) arises on account of metaphysical views of a roughly Aristotelian sort, the idea that the sperm, egg, or embryo has a *telos* or essence, such as that of the acorn whose essence lies in its potentiality to become an oak tree. Those who accept such a view usually also have a desire to bring about the said *telos*. Those who accept a naturalistic neo-Darwinian outlook on biology may deny the existence of such a *telos* or essence. We also have a desire not to desire the impossible. This higher order desire may therefore be canalized by a naturalistic metaphysics. Thus if someone comes through philosophical argument to accept a naturalistic metaphysics then he or she may come to lose the desire to oppose contraception or abortion, though he or she need not do so.

It is true that objection to contraception and abortion may be felt by a person who holds a quite neo-Darwinian and naturalistic outlook. Indeed in the case of abortion there is a natural repugnance at the thought of killing a foetus. This is partly like the repugnance that we might feel at making an incision into human flesh, which a person who has a higher order desire to become a surgeon will attempt to overcome, but the repugnance may also depend very reasonably on consequential considerations about the deprivation of the future happiness that would be possessed by the foetus in later life if it were allowed to live. The question of course is whether this consideration is outweighed by other considerations on the other side. Analogously, in the case of contraception, it can very plausibly be argued that one of the greatest potential threats to future happiness on the whole is overpopulation. There is presumably an optimum population of the world that can be achieved only by means of birth control. These are considerations both pro and con that are open to us if we reject the metaphysics of telos and essence. I am concerned here merely to give one more instance of how metaphysical considerations can be important to ethics, and how metaphysical beliefs may canalize desires in the manner suggested in Chapter 3. This is independent of whether metaphysics is continuous with science (as I myself believe it is). Either way it is factual and lies on the belief side of the belief/desire dichotomy.

NOTES

CHAPTER I INTRODUCTION

1 See J.J.C Smart, 'An outline of a system of utilitarian ethics', in J.J.C. Smart and Bernard Williams, *Utilitarianism: For and Against* (Cambridge University Press, 1973).
2 This point was well put to me in discussion by Helen Nissenbaum.
3 Roger Wertheimer, *The Significance of Sense* (Ithaca, New York: Cornell University Press, 1972).
4 W.V. Quine, *From a Logical Point of View*, 2nd edn (Cambridge, Mass.: Harvard University Press, 1961), especially Chapter 2, and *Word and Object* (Cambridge, Mass.: MIT Press, 1960).
5 See Hilary Putnam, 'The analytic and the synthetic', in Putnam's *Philosophical Papers*, vol. 2, *Mind, Language and Reality* (Cambridge University Press, 1975).
6 For an aseptic account of the analyticity of such sentences as 'No bachelors are married' see W.V. Quine, *The Roots of Reference* (La Salle, Illinois: Open Court, 1974), pp. 78-80.
7 G.E. Moore, *Principia Ethica* (Cambridge University Press, 1903).
8 Richard Price, *A Review of the Principal Questions in Morals*, edited by D. Daiches Raphael (Oxford: Clarendon Press, 1948).
9 For a discussion of many of these writers, see A.N. Prior, *Logic and the Basis of Ethics* (Oxford: Clarendon Press, 1949).
10 See C.L. Stevenson, *Ethics and Language* (New Haven: Yale University Press, 1944).
11 See R.M. Hare, *The Language of Morals* (Oxford: Clarendon Press, 1952; revised edn 1961).
12 Roger N. Hancock, *Twentieth Century Ethics* (New York: Columbia University Press, 1974).
13 G.J. Warnock, *The Object of Morality* (London: Methuen, 1971)
14 Philippa Foot, *Virtues and Vices and Other Essays in Moral Philosophy* (Berkeley and Los Angeles: University of California Press, 1978).

Notes to pages 8-12

15 R.M. Hare: *The Language of Morals* (Oxford: Clarendon Press, 1952); *Freedom and Reason* (Oxford: Clarendon Press, 1963); *Moral Thinking: Its Levels, Method and Point* (Oxford: Clarendon Press, 1981).
16 See Hare, *Moral Thinking*, pp. 91-2. Hare says that he is happy to accept such an extension. However he teasingly says 'vegetarians' to refer to those who advocate the extension of our concern beyond humans to other sentient beings. For those who do not notice the teasing, I want to say that one can be concerned for the happiness of animals without being a vegetarian. One may oppose factory farming without necessarily objecting to eating free range cattle, whose presumed surplus of pleasure to pain in their lives would not exist but for the fact that they were destined to be eaten. Also Hare's use of 'vegetarian' suggests concern for only terrestrial non-human sentient beings. We must surely extend our universal concern to non-terrestrial sentient beings, should we ever come into interaction with any of them, and I do not think that there would be any question of even a non-vegetarian ever wanting to *eat* some superior being from outer space!
17 Hare wishes to keep the formal requirement of universalizability and the putting of oneself in others' shoes as different moves in the argument. The latter is discussed in Chapter 5 of his *Moral Thinking* and the former in Chapter 6. See p. 108 of *Moral Thinking*.
18 See Hare, *Moral Thinking*, pp. 55-6.
19 Hare on p. 17 of *Moral Thinking* talks not only of preferences but of prescriptions. We may think that the former way of talking is better: after all it may make sense to say that a battery hen has a *preference* for not being de-beaked, not being confined, etc., but it is hard to know what to make of saying that the hen accepts *prescriptions*. However Hare defends the transition to talking of prescriptions on p. 107 of *Moral Thinking*.
20 *Moral Thinking*, p. 6.
21 *Moral Thinking*, p. 55.
22 D.H. Monro, *Empiricism and Ethics* (Cambridge University Press, 1967).
23 Joseph Butler, *Fifteen Sermons and Dissertation upon the Nature of Virtue*, edited by W.R. Matthews (London: Bell, 1953), Preface, para. 40.
24 On this question see Hare, *Moral Thinking*, pp. 112 ff.
25 Of course this is only an example from fiction, but it rings true as empirically plausible. Indeed the story was based in its fundamentals on a real case, that of Helen Walker, which was narrated in Scott's Introduction.
26 Here I use Quine's 'corner quotes'. $\ulcorner p \urcorner$ does not name a letter of the alphabet as does '*p*'. A schema containing '$\ulcorner p \urcorner$' and '*p*' instructs us to insert any sentence we like in place of the '*p*' and to insert the same sentence surrounded by quotation marks in place of the '$\ulcorner p \urcorner$'.

27 See, for example, Donald Davidson: 'Theories of meaning and learnable languages', in *Proceedings of the 1964 International Congress for Logic, Methodology and Philosophy of Science* (Amsterdam: North-Holland, 1965), pp. 383-94; 'Truth and meaning', *Synthese 17* (1967), pp. 304-23; 'Semantics for natural languages', *Linguaggi nella Società e nella Tecnica* (Milan: Edizioni di Communità, 1970), pp. 177-88.
28 See Davidson, 'Truth and meaning'.
29 I am assuming here that '⊃' captures the colloquial 'If . . . then . . .'. This is of course doubtful, but as I am here concerned with ethics and the distinction between imperatives and indicatives I shall here avoid buying into a discussion of the semantics of conditionals in colloquial language.
30 H.P. Grice, 'The causal theory of perception', *Proceedings of the Aristotelian Society*, supp. vol. 35 (1961), pp. 121-68.
31 For a good discussion of these matters see R.M. Hare, 'Some alleged differences between imperatives and indicatives', *Mind* 76 (1967), pp. 309-26. These matters are controversial. For a discussion of various points of view see Jonathan Bennett's review in *Journal of Symbolic Logic* 35 (1970), pp. 314-18, and the literature there mentioned.
32 Howard Burdick, 'A logical form for the propositional attitudes', *Synthese* 52 (1982), pp. 185-230.
33 Donald Davidson, 'On saying that', *Synthese 19* (1968-9), pp. 130-46.
34 See G. Adrian Horridge, 'Mechanistic teleology and explanation in neuroethology', *BioScience* 27 (1977), pp. 725-32.

CHAPTER II INTERLUDE ON THE NATURALISTIC FALLACY

1 W.K. Frankena, 'The naturalistic fallacy', *Mind* 48 (1939), pp. 464-77.
2 A.C. Ewing, 'A suggested non-naturalistic analysis of "Good"', *Mind* 48 (1939), pp. 1-22.
3 R.M. Hare, *The Language of Morals* (Oxford: Clarendon Press, 1952, revised edn 1961).
4 See Frank Jackson, 'Defining the autonomy of ethics', *Philosophical Review* 83 (1974), pp. 88-96, and papers by A.N. Prior, David R. Kurtzman and Max Black, referred to in Jackson's paper.
5 See J.M. Shorter, 'Professor Prior on the autonomy of ethics', *Australasian Journal of Philosophy* 39 (1961), pp. 286-7.
6 Frank Jackson, 'Defining the autonomy of ethics', *loc. cit.*
7 Donald Davidson, 'The logical form of action sentences', in Donald Davidson, *Essays on Actions and Events* (Oxford: Clarendon Press, 1980).
8 Donald Davidson, 'Psychology and philosophy', *loc. cit.*
9 W.V. Quine, *Word and Object* (Cambridge, Mass.: MIT Press, 1960).

10 On principles of charity see N.L. Wilson, 'Substances without substrata', review of *Metaphysics* 12 (1959), pp. 521-39; W.V. Quine, *Word and Object* (Cambridge, Mass.: MIT Press, 1960); Donald Davidson, 'Belief and the basis of meaning', *Synthese* 27 (1974), pp. 309-23; David Lewis, 'Radical interpretation', *ibid.*, pp. 331-44; W.V. Quine, 'Comment on Donald Davidson', *ibid.*, pp. 325-9; Donald Davidson, 'Replies to David Lewis and W.V. Quine', *ibid.*, pp. 345-9. Also importantly relevant is Howard Burdick's account of interpretation, as summarized on p. 250 of F.B. D'Agostino with H.R. Burdick, 'Symbolism and literalism in anthropology', *Synthese* 52 (1982), pp. 233-65.
11 As in C.L. Stevenson, *Ethics and Language* (New Haven: Yale University Press, 1944).
12 A.N. Prior, *Logic and the Basis of Ethics* (Oxford: Clarendon Press, 1949). Ernest and Maria Clark, 'What is goodness?', *Australasian Journal of Psychology and Philosophy* 19 (1941), pp. 144-64.
13 David Wiggins, 'Truth, invention and the meaning of life', *Proceedings of the British Academy* 62 (1976), pp. 331-78. John McDowell, 'Non-cognitivism and rule following', in Steven H. Holtzman and Christopher M. Leich (eds), *Wittgenstein: To Follow a Rule* (London: Routledge & Kegan Paul, 1981). Mark Platts, *Ways of Meaning* (London: Routledge & Kegan Paul, 1979), Chapter 10, and 'Moral reality and the end of desire', in Mark Platts (ed.), *Reference, Truth and Reality* (London: Routledge & Kegan Paul, 1980).
14 See F. Waismann, 'Verifiability', *Proceedings of the Aristotelian Society*, supp. vol. 19 (1945), pp. 119-50.
15 Wiggins, *op. cit.* For Wittgenstein on 'Following a rule', see L. Wittgenstein, *Remarks on the Foundations of Mathematics*, 3rd edn (Oxford: Blackwell, 1978).
16 See L. Wittgenstein, *Philosophical Investigations*, 3rd edn (Oxford: Blackwell, 1967), para. 65, D.A.T. Gasking, 'Clusters', *Australasian Journal of Philosophy* 38 (1960), pp. 1-36.
17 Wiggins, *op. cit.*, p. 348.
18 I should mention here the excellent critique of the emotive theory in J.O. Urmson, *The Emotive Theory of Ethics* (London: Hutchinson, 1968). (This book also contains interesting positive suggestions in ethical theory.)
19 A.J. Ayer, *Language, Truth and Logic*, 2nd edn (London: Gollancz, 1946), pp. 107-8.
20 Stevenson, *op. cit.*, Chapter 2.
21 Gilbert Ryle, *The Concept of Mind* (London: Hutchinson, 1949), Chapter 4.
22 *Concise Oxford Dictionary of Current English* (Oxford: Clarendon Press, 1964).
23 Ryle, *loc. cit.*
24 'Truth theory' sounds ugly, but I prefer to use it when referring it to a Davidsonian theory in which T-sentences are provable from axioms, and to use 'theory of truth', to indicate wider and more

traditional concerns, e.g. of whether truth is purely disquotational, as in Tarski, or whether it needs to be supplemented by other notions, such as that of correspondence to non-linguistic fact.
25 See David Lewis, 'Radical interpretation', *op. cit.*
26 R.M. Hare, *The Language of Morals, op. cit.*, p. 177.
27 C.L. Stevenson, *op. cit.*, p. 99.

CHAPTER III WHY MORAL LANGUAGE?

1 M. Zimmerman, 'The "is-ought" barrier: an unnecessary dualism', *Mind* 71 (1962), pp. 53-61, reprinted in W.D. Hudson (ed.), *The Is-Ought Question* (London, Macmillan, 1972). Also reprinted in this volume is Kenneth Hanley's discussion note, 'Zimmerman's is-is: a schizophrenic monism', *Mind* 73 (1964), pp. 443-5, and Zimmerman's reply, 'A note on the is-ought barrier', *Mind* 76 (1967), pp. 53-62.
2 Elizabeth Anscombe, 'Modern moral philosophy', *Philosophy* 33 (1958), pp. 1-19, reprinted in W.D. Hudson, *The Is-Ought Question, op. cit.* Anscombe holds that the language of 'ought' and 'right' is a survival from a notion of divine law, so that in modern secular society it has survived after the framework of thought that made it intelligible has collapsed. However Anscombe would not extend this account to all ethical discourse. In the just-mentioned article she hints at a somewhat Aristotelian theory of ethics. Philippa Foot in her 'Morality as a system of hypothetical imperatives', *Philosophical Review* 81 (1972), pp. 305-16, speaks of those who emphatically close off discussion of the moral 'ought' as relying on an illusion, as if giving the moral 'ought' a magic force (p. 315). This paper is reprinted in Philippa Foot, *Virtues and Vices* (Berkeley and Los Angeles: University of California Press, 1978). See p. 167.
3 J.L. Mackie, *Ethics: Inventing Right and Wrong* (Harmondsworth: Penguin Books, 1977), especially pp. 42-5. See also J.L. Mackie, 'The refutation of morals', *Australasian Journal of Philosophy* 24 (1946), pp. 77-90.
4 J.J.C. Smart: *Philosophy and Scientific Realism* (London: Routledge & Kegan Paul, 1963); 'Reports of immediate experiences', *Synthese* 22 (1971), pp. 346-59; 'On some criticisms of a physicalist theory of colors', in Chung-ying Cheng (ed.), *Philosophical Aspects of the Mind-Body Problem* (Honolulu: University Press of Hawaii, 1975).
5 J.L. Mackie, *Inventing Right and Wrong, op. cit.*, p. 44.
6 H.P. Grice's expression. See H.P. Grice, 'Logic and conversation', an extract from Grice's William James Lectures at Harvard University, in Donald Davidson and Gilbert Harman (eds), *The Logic of Grammar* (Encino and Belmont, California: Dickenson Publishing Company, 1975).
7 Richard Ballantine, *Richard's Bicycle Book*, new revised and expanded edition (London: Pan Books, 1979). See p. 260.

8 Immanuel Kant, *Groundwork of the Metaphysic of Morals*, English translation by H.J. Paton under the title *The Moral Law* (London: Hutchinson, 1948), pp. 82 ff.
9 J.L. Austin, 'Ifs and cans', in his *Philosophical Papers*, edited by J.O. Urmson and G.J. Warnock (Oxford: Clarendon Press, 1961).
10 John C. Harsanyi, 'Ethics in terms of hypothetical imperatives', *Mind* 67 (1958), pp. 305-16, reprinted in his *Essays on Ethics, Social Behavior, and Scientific Explanation* (Dordrecht: D. Reidel, 1976). Philippa Foot, 'Morality as a system of hypothetical imperatives', in *Virtues and Vices, op. cit.*
11 John McDowell, 'Are moral requirements hypothetical imperatives?' *Aristotelian Society*, supp. vol. 52 (1978), pp. 13-29. See p. 15.
12 This indicates also how I would reply to an argument by Thomas Nagel, in his book *The Possibility of Altruism* (Oxford: Clarendon Press, 1970), pp. 28 ff. Nagel holds that in some cases to ascribe a desire is to do no more than say that someone acted in a certain way. This is like saying that to say that the girder had metal fatigue is to say nothing over and above the assertion that the girder collapsed. Nagel says that we can ascribe a desire purely on the basis of behaviour but then it is 'only a logically necessary condition of behaviour'. So such an ascription of desire is taken by Nagel to be empty. But in view of Quine's criticism of analyticity such a reliance on the notion of logical necessity is problematical. Moreover even if it were a logical necessity that my mother bore me, that would not show that my mother was not a cause of my birth!
13 Donald Davidson, *Essays on Actions and Events* (Oxford: Clarendon Press, 1980), p. 6. Aristotle uses the word '*orexis*'. R.M. Hare mentions this matter in his 'Ethical theory and utilitarianism', in H.D. Lewis (ed.), *Contemporary British Philosophy* 4 (London: Allen & Unwin, 1976). See p. 121.
14 Joseph Butler, *Fifteen Sermons, Preached at the Rolls Chapel and a Dissertation Upon the Nature of Virtue*, with Introduction, Analyses and Notes by the Very Rev. W.R. Matthews (London: G. Bell & Sons, 1953). See Sermon I.
15 For a modern defence of the desire-belief model of explanation, see Andrew Woodfield, *Teleology* (Cambridge University Press, 1976), pp. 166 ff.
16 Winston Nesbitt, 'Categorical imperatives: a defense', *Philosophical Review* 86 (1977), pp. 217-25.
17 Winston Leonard Spencer Nesbitt, *An Objectivist Account of Morals*, PhD Thesis, University of Adelaide, 1977. I am very grateful to Nesbitt for his permission to discuss Chapters 10 and 11 of his thesis.
18 Donald Regan, *Utilitarianism and Co-operation* (Oxford: Clarendon Press, 1980).
19 B.C. Postow has suggested that act utilitarianism be modified so as to apply to groups, in his 'Generalized act utilitarianism', *Analysis* 37 (1977), pp. 49-52.
20 J.S. Mill, 'Utilitarianism', Chapter 4, in J.S Mill, *On Liberty, Essay*

on Bentham, together with *Selected Writings of Jeremy Bentham and John Austin*, ed. Mary Warnock (London: Macmillan, 1962).
21 John Kilcullen has developed Mills's insight in an interesting way. See John Kilcullen, 'Utilitarianism and virtue', *Ethics* 93 (1982-3), pp. 451-66.
22 For an account of the sort of co-operation required see Donald Regan's book, *op. cit.*

CHAPTER IV CONSIDERATIONS ABOUT THE SEMANTICS OF 'OUGHT'

1 See the extract from Samuel Clarke's 'Discourse on the unchangeable obligations of natural religion', 4th edn, 1716, reprinted in L.A. Selby-Bigge, *British Moralists*, vol. 2 (Oxford: Clarendon Press, 1897).
2 C.D. Broad, *Five Types of Ethical Theory* (London: Routledge & Kegan Paul, 1930), pp. 164-5; Sir David Ross, *Foundations of Ethics* (Oxford: Clarendon Press, 1939), pp. 51 ff.
3 On this matter see Donald Davidson, 'True to the facts', *Journal of Philosophy* 66 (1969), pp. 748-64. See also P.F. Strawson, 'Truth', *Aristotelian Society*, supp. vol. 24 (1950), pp. 129-56, especially pp. 139-41.
4 Hector-Neri Castañeda, 'The paradoxes of deontic logic: the simplest solution to all of them in one fell swoop', in Risto Hilpenen (ed.), *New Studies in Deontic Logic* (Dordrecht: D. Reidel, 1981).
5 Bruce Vermazen, 'The logic of practical "ought"-sentences', *Philosophical Studies* 32 (1977), pp. 1-71. See also Eric Dayton, 'Two approaches to deontic logic', *Journal of Value Enquiry* 15 (1981), pp. 117-47.
6 *Op. cit.*
7 *Cf.* Vermazen, *op. cit.*, pp. 8-9.
8 For a 'possible worlds' approach to these, see David Lewis, *Counterfactuals* (Oxford: Blackwell, 1973). Those of us who dislike 'possible worlds' will need to deal with similar technical problems (of 'discounting evidence' and the like) in some way or other.
9 Roger Wertheimer, *The Significance of Sense: Meaning, Modality and Morality* (Ithaca: Cornell University Press, 1972).
10 See Bruce Vermazen's review of Wertheimer's *The Significance of Sense, Journal of Philosophy* 71 (1974), pp. 506-12.
11 See Donald Davidson, *Essays on Actions and Events* (Oxford: Clarendon Press, 1980), Chapter 8, 'The individuation of events'.
12 Vermazen, 'The logic of practical "ought"-sentences', p. 15.
13 Ross, *The Foundations of Ethics, op. cit.*, pp. 84-5.

CHAPTER V GOODNESS

1 See R.M. Hare, *The Language of Morals* (Oxford: Clarendon Press, 1952), pp. 96-9, P.T. Geach, 'Good and evil', *Analysis* 17 (1956-7) 33-42, and J.O. Urmson, *The Emotive Theory of Ethics* (London, Hutchinson, 1968), pp. 98-116.
2 For the notion of 'a complete novel' see Richard Jeffrey, *The Logic of Decision* (New York: McGraw Hill, 1965), pp. 196-7. For set theoretical surrogates see W.V. Quine, 'Propositional objects', in W.V. Quine, *Ontological Relativity* (New York: Columbia University Press, 1969) and David Lewis, *Counterfactuals* (Oxford: Blackwell, 1973), pp. 89-91.
3 See also R.M. Hare, *The Language of Morals* (Oxford: Clarendon Press, 1952), pp. 183-4.
4 For a detailed discussion of difficulties of this sort see Mark Platts, *Ways of Meaning* (London: Routledge & Kegan Paul, 1979), pp. 170-89.
5 C.L. Stevenson, *Ethics and Language* (New Haven: Yale University Press, 1944), Chapter 8.
6 As in David Lewis, *Convention* (Cambridge, Mass.: Harvard University Press, 1969) and *Counterfactuals*, *op. cit.*
7 For criticisms of 'satisfaction utilitarianism' see J.J.C. Smart, 'Hedonistic and ideal utilitarianism', *Midwest Studies in Philosophy* 3 (1978), pp. 240-51.

CHAPTER VI ETHICS, TRUTH AND FACT

1 L. Wittgenstein, *Tractatus Logico-Philosophicus*, with new translation by D.F. Pears and B.F. McGuinness, and with an Introduction by Bertrand Russell (London: Routledge & Kegan Paul, 1961).
2 See P.F. Strawson, 'Truth', *Aristotelian Society*, supp. vol. 24 (1950), pp. 129-56.
3 W.V. Quine, *The Roots of Reference* (La Salle, Illinois: Open Court, 1973), pp. 111-15.
4 Donald Davidson, 'True to the facts', *Journal of Philosophy* 66 (1969), pp. 748-64.
5 *Ibid.*, p. 753.
6 Barry Taylor, 'States of affairs', in Gareth Evans and John McDowell, *Truth and Meaning* (Oxford: Clarendon Press, 1976).
7 F.P. Ramsey, 'General propositions and causality', in F.P. Ramsey, *Foundations: Essays in Philosophy, Logic, Mathematics and Economics* edited by D.H. Mellor (London: Routledge & Kegan Paul, 1978). See p. 134.
8 D.M. Armstrong, *Belief, Truth and Knowledge* (Cambridge University Press, 1971), Part I.
9 John Perry, 'The problem of the essential indexical', *Noûs* 13 (1979), pp. 3-21. See also David Lewis, 'Attitudes *De Dicto and De Se*',

Philosophical Review 88 (1979), pp. 513-43.
10 As in the translation by Pears and McGuinness (see note 1).
11 Compare Roger Scruton, 'Truth conditions and criteria', *Aristotelian Society*, supp. vol. 50 (1976), pp. 193-216. This is part of a very good symposium with Crispin Wright, whose interesting reply to Scruton makes some criticisms that do not seem to me to affect the present point at issue as I have cautiously made it in the text.
12 I am indeed much in agreement with Simon Blackburn's defence of a sophisticated projection theory, in Blackburn's 'Rule following and moral realism', in Steven H. Holtzman and Christopher M. Leich, *Wittgenstein: To Follow a Rule* (London: Routledge & Kegan Paul, 1981). Blackburn's paper is a reply to John McDowell's 'Following a rule and ethics', in the same volume.
13 Consider the shocked reception in some quarters of C.L. Stevenson's *Ethics and Language* (New Haven: Yale University Press, 1944) when it was supposed that he was undermining morality. *Cf.* Brand Blanshard, *Reason and Analysis* (La Salle, Illinois: Open Court, 1962), p. 125 near top. Blanshard was well aware, however, that, as he put it, one cannot refute a meta-ethical analysis by pointing to unfortunate practical consequences of adopting it. My contention is that the worry is needless – the unfortunate practical consequences do not seem to me to exist. Adam Smith's letter is reprinted on pp. 604-5 of E.C. Mossner, *The Life of David Hume* (Oxford: Clarendon Press, 1970), which contains *passim* much other evidence of Hume's virtue, as indeed does in briefer compass Adam Smith's short letter.

CHAPTER VII 'OUGHT', 'CAN', FREE WILL AND RESPONSIBILITY

1 Bruce Vermazen, 'The logic of practical "ought"-sentences', *Philosophical Studies* 32 (1977), pp. 1-71. See pp. 62-3.
2 *Ibid.*, p. 40.
3 Marquis P.S. de Laplace, *A Philosophical Essay on Probabilities*, translated from the 6th French edition by F.W. Truscott and F.L. Emory (New York: Dover, 1951), p. 4.
4 Richard Montague, 'Deterministic theories', in Richard Montague, *Formal Philosophy*, edited and with an Introduction by Richmond H. Thomason (New Haven: Yale University Press, 1974).
5 See K.R. Popper, 'Indeterminism in quantum physics and in classical physics', *British Journal for the Philosophy of Science* I (1950-1), pp. 117-33 and 173-95. For an interesting critique of Popper's paper see Michael Radner, 'Popper and Laplace' in Michael Radner and Stephen Winokur (eds), *Analyses of Theories and Methods of Physics and Psychology*, *Minnesota Studies in the Philosophy of Science* IV (Minneapolis: University of Minnesota Press, 1970), pp. 417-27.
6 Compare also Gilbert Ryle, *The Concept of Mind* (London: Hutchinson, 1949), p. 197.

7 Richard Montague, 'Deterministic theories', *op. cit.* This model-theoretic approach also seems to me to circumvent a more recent and very interesting argument by Popper in his *The Open Universe, An Argument for Indeterminism* (London: Hutchinson, 1982), pp. 57-62. Popper points out that because of the finite constant velocity of light, and because no other influences can be propagated faster than light, a predictor can receive information only from some cross-section of its backwards light cone. Hence the predictor can at most retrodict, not predict. But future events can be influenced from outside the predictor's backwards light cone, since the future event's backwards light cone includes the predictor's one. Here Popper is of course concerned with a matter of principle: in practice we can generally discount the very distant influences from outside the light cone at some earlier time. Incidentally I find Popper's stress on prediction in his account of determinism and indeterminism a little surprising, in view of his valiant and admirable opposition to verificationism and positivism. Unfortunately I saw this argument of Popper's only very recently: books can take a long time to reach Australia by slow boat, and I was only very belatedly aware that the above-mentioned interesting and readable book by Popper had even been published.

8 See Ernest Nagel, *The Structure of Science*, (New York: Harcourt, Brace & World, 1961), pp. 278-93.

9 J.L. Mackie has defined a cause as an INUS condition, i.e. as 'an *insufficient* but *necessary* part of a condition which is iself *unnecessary* but *sufficient* for the result'. See J.L. Mackie, 'Causes and conditions', *American Philosophical Quarterly* 2 (1965), pp. 245-61. For an acute criticism see F.C. Jackson's review of various papers on causality, *Journal of Symbolic Logic* 47 (1982), pp. 470-3.

10 R.E. Hobart, 'Free-will as involving determinism and inconceivable without it', *Mind* 43 (1934), pp. 1-27.

11 In a forthcoming paper.

12 See C.A. Campbell, 'Is free-will a pseudo-problem?', *Mind* 60 (1951), pp. 441-65, and 'Professor Smart on Free-will, praise and blame: a reply', *Mind* 72 (1963), pp. 400-5. The latter is a reply to J.J.C. Smart, 'Free-will, praise and blame', *Mind* 70 (1961), pp. 291-306. See also William H. Halverson, 'The bogy of chance: a reply to Professor Smart', *Mind* 73 (1964), pp. 567-70. But see also J.J.C. Smart, 'Philosophy and scientific plausibility', in Paul K. Feyerabend and Grover Maxwell (eds), *Mind Matter and Method, Essays in Philosophy and Science in Honor of Herbert Feigl* (Minneapolis: University of Minnesota Press, 1966).

13 For hints towards a possible psychological explanation of why Campbell should feel that he can introspect that he has contra-casual freedom, see Hume's *Treatise*, bk II, pt III, sec. 2, para. 2.

14 D.M. McKay, 'Brain and will', *Listener* 57 (1957), pp. 788-9.

15 Karl R. Popper and John C. Eccles, *The Self and its Brain* (Berlin: Springer, 1977). See p. 477.

16 Gerald Feinberg, 'Physics and the Thales problem', *Journal of*

Philosophy 63 (1966), pp. 5-17.
17 On Popper's 'three worlds' see Karl R. Popper, *Objective Knowledge* (Oxford: The Clarendon Press, 1972), and Karl R. Popper and John C. Eccles, *The Self and its Brain*, *op. cit.*, and Karl R. Popper, *The Open Universe*, *op. cit.*, pp. 113-30.
18 Perhaps Popper agrees here. See near bottom of p. 128 of his *The Open Universe*. I may have understood Popper's World 3 too Platonistically. But if I have, then I am even more in the dark about how World 3 is supposed by Popper to bear on the question of free will.

CHAPTER VIII ETHICS, SCIENCE AND METAPHYSICS

1 Peter Singer, *Animal Liberation: A New Ethics for Our Treatment of Animals* (New York: Random House, 1975).
2 See John Passmore, 'The treatment of animals', *Journal of the History of Ideas* 36 (1975), pp. 195-218, especially p. 200. Compare 'The life of Brother Juniper', Chapter 1, in *The Little Flowers of St Francis and Other Franciscan Writings*, translated by S. Hughes (New York: Mentor-Omega Books, 1964).
3 See the long footnote to paragraph 4 of Section 1 of Chapter XVII of Jeremy Bentham's *Principles of Morals and Legislation*.
4 See J.J.C. Smart, 'My semantic ascents and descents', in Charles J. Bontempo and S. Jack Odell, *The Owl of Minerva* (New York: McGraw-Hill, 1975). The lack of a sharp line between science and metaphysics is of course fundamental in the thought of W.V. Quine (at least if metaphysics is properly done and is not the attempt to deduce facts about the world purely *a priori*).
5 William James, *The Will to Believe* (New York: Longmans Green, 1897), p. 188. Ursula K. Le Guin has written a moving story, 'The ones who walk away from Omelas, variations on a theme by William James'. See Ursula K. Le Guin, *The Wind's Twelve Quarters*, vol. 2 (London: Granada (Panther), 1980).
6 See H. Sidgwick, *The Methods of Ethics*, 7th edn (Chicago University Press, 1962), pp. 418-19; Derek Parfit, 'Later selves and moral principles', in Alan Montefiore (ed.), *Philosophy and Personal Relations: an Anglo-French Study* (London: Routledge & Kegan Paul, 1973), pp. 137-69; J.J.C. Smart, 'Utilitarianism and Justice', *Chinese Journal of Philosophy* 5 (1978), pp. 287-99, especially p. 293, and 'Distributive justice and utilitarianism', in John Arthur and William H. Shaw (eds), *Justice and Economic Distribution* (Englewood Cliffs, New Jersey: Prentice-Hall, 1978), pp. 103-15.
7 On this subject see Peter Singer, *The Expanding Circle* (Oxford: Clarendon Press, 1981).
8 Even less relevant to the question of factuality is the subjectivity (often stressed by sociologists) arising out of the selection of what to

study or of where to put research funds. There may be subjectivity in such selective attention to facts, but that has nothing to do with the question of the factuality of these facts.

9 Renford Bambrough has made interesting relevant comparisons between theoretical thinking and practical thinking. See Renford Bambrough, *Moral Scepticism and Moral Knowledge* (London: Routledge & Kegan Paul, 1979), especially pp. 18-19.

10 Consider for example the literature arising out of Bell's inequality.

11 H.J. Groenewold, 'Modern science and social responsibility', in Paul Weingartner and Gerhard Zecha (eds), *Induction, Physics and Ethics, Proceedings and Discussions of the 1968 Salzburg Colloquium in the Philosophy of Science* (Dordrecht: D. Reidel, 1970).

12 Other important macro effects will of course arise if we succeed in averting nuclear war. One will come from our ability through genetic engineering to control the evolution of the species. This, together with other biological abilities, such as the ability to control the proportion of male and female children, *in vitro* fertilization, artificial wombs and cloning, will surely give rise to agonizing moral questioning.

13 But see J.J.C. Smart, 'The reality of the future', *Philosophia* 10 (1981), pp. 141-50.

14 In the volume mentioned in note 11. See p. 368.

15 Similarly I have heard it said that the objection to killing whales is the pain they suffer in being killed, whereas I should want to say that it is the future happiness of which they are deprived that is also important (and the future happiness that their descendants who are deprived of existence would have had).

16 My brother Ninian Smart once used this as a *reductio ad absurdum* of this sort of negative utilitarianism. See R.N. Smart, 'Negative utilitarianism', *Mind* 67 (1958), pp. 542-3.

17 See remarks by Yehoshua Bar-Hillel in the volume mentioned in note 11, on p. 372.

INDEX

Affective 'ought', 81
Analyticity, 4-5, 104
Analytic philosophy, 1-3
Animals, 129
Anscombe, Elizabeth, 51, 148
Anthropology, 30-3
Aristotle, 7, 121, 142
Armstrong, D.M., 99
Attitude theory, 39-40
Austen, Jane, 39
Austin, J.L., 57, 77
Ayer, A.J., 38-9

Beliefs, 30, 47, 50, 55, 59, 97-9
Benn, Stanley, 9
Bentham, Jeremy, 129-30
Blackburn, Simon, 152
Borrow, George, 137
Broad, C.D., 65
Burdick, Howard, 19
Butler, Joseph, 10, 58

Campbell, C.A., 121-4
Cantor, G., 95
Cartesian dualism, 125
Castañeda, H.-N., 68
Causal chains, 112-13, 121
Cawkwell, G.L., 104
Clark, Ernest and Maria, 34, 36
Clarke, Samuel, 65

Conation, 58
Contra-causal freedom, 121-3
Cook, Captain James, 30
Co-operation, 60-3
Correspondence theory, 95

Dalton, J., 60
Davidson, Donald, 13-14, 19, 30-1, 58, 75, 85-6, 95-6, 105
Deans, Effie, 11
Deans, Jeanie, 11-12, 99, 102
Definist fallacy, 23-4
Deontic logic, 67-9
Desires, 10, 31, 37, 50, 52, 55, 60, 102-5, 120, 122, 138, 142-3
Determinism, 107, 108-14
Dirac, P.A.M., 132
Dummett, Michael, 13

Eccles, Sir John, 114, 125
Egoism, 8, 136
Einstein, A., 132
Emotivism, 29, 33, 36, 38-44
Epistemic 'ought', 54, 64, 69
Evaluation, 90-3
Ewing, A.C., 24

Facts, 49, 53, 94-7
Feinberg, G., 125
Fittingness, 65-6

Index

Foot, Philippa, 8, 57-8, 60-2
Frankena, W.K., 23-4
Future, 140-2

Galileo Galilei, 133
God, 11, 84, 99, 129, 137
Gödel, Kurt, 13
Golden rule, 129, 133
Good Samaritan paradox, 67-8, 81
Grice, H.P., 18, 93
Groenewold, H.J., 139-41

Hancock, Roger N., 8
Hare, R.M., 2, 8-10, 26, 43, 80
Harsanyi, J.C., 57
Hobart, R.E., 114
Hobbes, Thomas, 62
Hume, David, 6, 20, 26, 39, 98, 102, 103-4, 121, 136
Hypothetical imperatives, 57

Imperatives, 14-19, 29, 42, 50, 97
Indeterminism, 113-14, 153
Inquisition, 133
Intrinsic and extrinsic preferences, 87-90
Is-ought barrier, 45-50

Jackson, Frank, 27-9, 117, 119
James, William, 134-6
Jeffrey, Richard, 85, 89

Kant, Immanuel, 7, 57
Kilcullen, John, 61
Kripke, Saul, 96

Laplace, Marquis P.S. de, 109, 112
Lewis, David, 88, 108, 148
Lysenko, T.D., 133

McDowell, John, 57-8, 143
MacKay, D.M., 124
Mackie, J.L., 51-3, 102-4
Maps, 97-101
Meaning, 3-6, 12, 31, 56
Mental illness, 119
Meta-ethics, 7-8, 30, 141

Metaphysics, 7, 138-43
Mill, J.S., 61
Monro, D.H., 10
Moore, G.E., 4-6, 22-6, 29, 33, 37, 49, 52, 72, 82, 87-9, 91, 103

Nagel, Thomas, 149
Naturalism, 22, 33
Naturalistic fallacy, 4-6, 22-9
Nesbitt, W.L.S., 60-2
Newton, Isaac, 20
Nissenbaum, Helen, 72
Normative ethics, 7

Perry, John, 99
Personal identity, 136
Persuasion, 21, 44-8, 90-1
Plan, 74-9, 81, 107
Platts, Mark, 147
Popper, Sir Karl, 125-6, 153
Possible worlds, 85, 87-9
Pragmatics, 19, 64, 90, 106
Praise and blame, 114-19
Predicate modifier, 83-6
Price, Richard, 4
Prichard, H.A., 4
Prima facie duty, 80
Prior, A.N., 34
Progress in ethics and science, 128-34
Projection theory, 52-3, 102-3

Quine, W.V., 4-6, 19, 29-30, 33, 64, 83, 85-6, 95

Radical translation and interpretation, 29-34, 41
Ramsey, F.P., 99
Rawls, John, 7
Regan, Donald, 60
Responsibility, 116-20
Rhetoric, 48, 134-8
Ross, Sir David, 65, 72, 80
Ryle, Gilbert, 39

Scott, Sir Walter, 5, 11, 105
Scruton, Roger, 152

Index

Semantics, 12-19, 40, 42, 64-86, 90, 92-3, 94-7, 102, 103, 106
Sidgwick, H., 7
Singer, Peter, 129, 134
Smith, Adam, 104
Socrates, 136
Stevenson, C.L., 38-9, 43-4, 88
Stevenson, R.L., 99
Strahan, William, 104
Subjective betterness, 69-70
Subjectivism, 33-4, 36
Supervenience, 35-7

Tarski, A., 12-14, 17, 18, 31, 94-9
Taylor, Barry, 96-7
Teresa, Mother, 132
Truth, 12-14, 94-6
Truth theory, 12-14

Urmson, J.O., 39
Utilitarianism, 62, 79-80, 134-6

Vegetarians, 145
Vermazen, Bruce, 68-9, 71, 73-6, 78-9, 106-8
Vetter, Hermann, 141

Warnock, G.J., 8
Wertheimer, Roger, 4, 71
Wiggins, David, 37, 147
Wittgenstein, L., 100-1, 124
World 1, World 2, World 3, 126
Wright, Crispin, 152

Zimmerman, M., 45-8, 50-1, 54, 57-8

For Product Safety Concerns and Information please contact our EU
representative GPSR@taylorandfrancis.com
Taylor & Francis Verlag GmbH, Kaufingerstraße 24, 80331 München, Germany

www.ingramcontent.com/pod-product-compliance
Lightning Source LLC
Chambersburg PA
CBHW052128300426
44116CB00010B/1812